The Book of Banbury 1975
has been published as a
Limited Edition of which
this is

Number 3 4 3

A complete list of the
original subscribers is
printed at the back of
the book.

THE BOOK OF BANBURY

The early 19th century view of the South Bar and Market Place.

THE BOOK OF BANBURY

AN ILLUSTRATED RECORD

BY

CHRISTINE BLOXHAM, BA, AMA

With best wishes,
Christine Bloxham

BARRACUDA BOOKS LIMITED
CHESHAM, BUCKINGHAMSHIRE, ENGLAND

MCMLXXV

PUBLISHED BY BARRACUDA BOOKS LIMITED

CHESHAM, ENGLAND

AND PRINTED BY

MALCOLM G. READ LIMITED

175 BERMONDSEY STREET

LONDON SE1

BOUND BY

BOOKBINDERS OF LONDON LIMITED

LONDON N5

JACKET PRINTED BY

WHITE CRESCENT PRESS LIMITED

LUTON, ENGLAND

LITHOGRAPHY BY

SOUTH MIDLANDS LITHO PLATES LIMITED

LUTON, ENGLAND

TYPE SET IN

MONOTYPE BASKERVILLE SERIES 169

BY SOUTH BUCKS TYPESETTERS LIMITED

BEACONSFIELD, ENGLAND

ISBN 0 86023 007 4

Contents

Acknowledgements

Many people have given me much help and support in writing this book; I am most grateful to them all. Above all, my photographer, Jon Hall, has spent many long hours painstakingly copying, photographing and printing to produce these excellent results. Crispin Paine helped me work out a framework for the book, and planned the 'Walkabout'; E. T. Clark, former editor of the Banbury Guardian, generously agreed to write 'Banbury Today' a subject I could not have tackled without his insight; Dr E. R. C. Brinkworth, who has a wide knowledge of Banbury history has given me advice and encouragement; my mother has patiently deciphered my illegible scrawl to type the manuscript and my father has drawn the pictures for the cover and endpapers; The Banbury Historical Society has given me its support; Peter Lock of Bloxham School compiled and drew the archaeological maps and helped publicise the book; Mr M. Draper, David McClaughlin and Rob Chilcott have provided original drawings, John Cheney has generously allowed me to use his firm's archives, Clive Birch, my publisher has been very patient with me and helped me out of my difficulties. I am also particularly indebted to Lord Saye & Sele, Mr J. Wells, Oxfordshire County Chief Librarian; Mr F. Parry, Librarian of Banbury Library; Mary Stanton of Banbury Museum; Cherwell District Council, General Foods, Alcan Booth, Banbury Guardian, Oxford Mail, Focus and Banbury Cake, Mrs Kirsty Rodwell of the Oxfordshire Archaeological Unit, Harry Judge, formerly headmaster of Banbury School and now director of the Oxford University Department of Educational Studies, Gaby Porter, Sir Spencer Summers, John Rhodes, Mrs C. Hughes, John Portergill, John Roberts, Rev I. Beecham, R. A. Foster, Dianne Coles, Jeremy Gibson, Derek Barrett, South Northampton-shire Archaeological Society, Andrew Sherratt, Christopher Hone, James Bond, Martin Blinkhorn, David Smith and Mary Clappinson.

In addition to the photographs specifically acknowledged in the text, Ashmolean Museum, Oxford and Bodleian Library, Oxford have enabled me to use copyright material.

Dedication

To my Mother and Father

Foreword

by Lord Saye and Sele

Alfred Beesley's solid History of Banbury published as long ago as 1841 and William Potts' briefer history, written in the first half of this century, are the two principal records of Banbury history. To these illustrious names can now be added that of Christine Bloxham, author of The Book of Banbury, a pictorial record of the town and district. It contains many fascinating photographs of Banbury all described in a lively and very readable manner.

Christine Bloxham who was for some years assistant at the Banbury Museum is now Assistant Keeper of Antiquities at the Oxfordshire County Museum and is Honorary Secretary of the Banbury Historical Society.

This history is an essential companion to Beesley and Potts and one which will give lasting pleasure to present and future Banburians.

BROUGHTON CASTLE.
August 1975.

Saye & Sele.

Preface

by Dr E. R. C. Brinkworth

Miss Christine Bloxham has assembled a mass of highly useful and entertaining illustrations of bygone Banbury. To accompany these she has written a delightfully palatable commentary.

This is the first time any collection of pictures has been made for the history of Banbury. Thus we have here a volume which is unique. It should certainly prove popular. It will provide the lucky possessor with a volume to which he can turn again and again. He will find it of lasting value and a source of abiding pleasure.

BANBURY.
August 1975.

E. R. C. Brinkworth

9

Crouch Hill

— a descriptive poem

But see where o'er the rest, with nobler blaze,
Its eight crown'd turrets Banbury displays
Upon its hallow'd walls, and wide around
Thick rising structures occupy the ground,
Here to the west Bull-Bar its front extends,
To Warwick north, the south to Oxford lands,
The East to the Canal; and spreading near
Rich gardens, fertile meads, and fields appear.
Behold now Phebus with his early lights
Shines on the battlements, and builded heights.
High o'er the roofs the curling smoke aspires,
Expanding as it leaves the genial fires.
Here flourish manufactories and arts,
And num'rous workmen ply their useful parts;
Swift fly the pointed shuttles thr' the looms,
And moving beams reverb'rate round the rooms.
Quick industry, with busy air and face,
Presides o'er all, and moves from place to place.
By persevering care are fortunes made.
And wealthy men more wealthy grow by trade.
We turn to the Canal, whose level flood
Now wets the bounds where once the Castle stood;
Of all its ancient consequence bereft,
To ruin fall'n, and scarce a vestige left.
The marks in which the moat begirt the pile
Alone remain upon th'indented foil;
The rest to dark oblivion long a prey,
Alas! how human grandeur fades away!
No more its iron bulwarks now it boasts
With which it us'd to awe surrounding hosts,
And guard the country; all its honors fled;
Where now the terror its possessors spread!

Philip Rusher (1789)

Goodly Faire

'Banbury is a goodly faire Market towne, and it is famous for Cakes, Cheese and Zeale.' Thus wrote John Taylor, the 'Water Poet' in 1636. Its position in the midst of a rich farming area led to the importance of its markets and fairs, which in turn stimulated local crafts and industries such as webbing and girth manufacture, thus serving the surrounding area.

The town and church were closely connected. As an administrative centre for the Bishop of Lincoln from the 11th century, it had a magnificent church and substantial castle, visited by monarchs throughout the mediaeval, Tudor and Stuart periods. Yet the town's Puritan zeal led to the destruction of its famous crosses and to notoriety in literature.

Major 19th century industries—plush manufacture and new agricultural machines—served worldwide markets, as much due to indigenous wit and skills as to the communications explosion brought about by the railway revolution, which brought the town into closer contact with the outside world.

Banbury people have always been individualists, holding themselves somewhat apart from the rest of the county. Characters such as William Whately, the Puritan Divine, and Bernhard Samuelson, the industrialist, flourished here, together with 'Old Mettle', the matchseller and Thomas Colley, the 'Banbury Pedestrian'.

Banbury's outward face has changed dramatically over the centuries, and not always for the better, with the destruction of the crosses, castle, church and cake shop. Nevertheless, the town's past—people, places and events—together weave a rich and exciting tapestry.

MARRIAGE
OF THE
PRINCESS ROYAL.

MANY of the respectable and influential Inhabitants of the Town hearing with regret that, instead of some lasting memorial being erected in the town to celebrate the Marriage of the Princess Royal, a subscription has been set on foot for a Ball only, by which any money that may be subscribed will be frittered away to no lasting good; ask their fellow-townsmen to pause before they subscribe to so paltry a way of showing their loyalty on this occasion. Let an historical cross, or some other substantial memorial, be erected, which will not only do honour to the occasion, but be a lasting credit and honour to the town.

ABOVE LEFT: William Knight helped to destroy Banbury's crosses.

BELOW LEFT: Plea to build a cross (Banbury Library).

RIGHT: Banbury bookmark (Banbury Museum).

Ride a Cock Horse

Ride a cock horse to Banbury Cross,
To see a fine lady upon a white horse,
With rings on her fingers and bells on her toes,
She shall have music wherever she goes.

The earliest musical and literary experience for most English children includes this well loved rhyme, which is all some people ever learn of Banbury. The rhyme was handed down as part of oral tradition, and the first published version, of 1744, was very different to the one learnt as a child:

'Ride a cock horse
To Banbury Cross
To see what Tommy can buy,
A Penny White Loaf,
A Penny White Cake,
And a Hugegy penny pie.'

In some versions 'a twopenny Apple pie' ends the rhyme. Hugegy presumably means enormous. Two versions refer to Banbury's great horse fair, which was held each January:

'Ride a cock horse to Banbury Cross,
To buy little Johnny a galloping horse,
It trots behind and it ambles before,
And Johnny shall ride till he can ride no more.'

and

'Hight o-cock horse, to Banbury Cross,
To buy a new nag and nimble horse.'

These versions are closely linked with everyday life and the important family event—a visit to the market.

It has been suggested that the rhyme reflected pagan rites when a lady rode in procession round the fields in the Spring to ensure good crops. Christianity turned the lady from a goddess into a May Queen, and her procession to Rogationtide. The rings symbolised power and the bells plenty. Certainly the horse was sacred in pagan times—the white horse carved in the hill at Uffington is not far away, and a red horse was carved in the ironstone near Edgehill. 'Ride a cock horse' seemed to historian William Potts to suggest a man and a woman riding one horse, as pictured in mediaeval manuscripts. The 'cock horse' has also been interpreted as a child's hobby horse. Telling evidence against this romantic interpretation is the lack of any knowledge of the rhyme before the mid 18th century, and the more mundane variations.

13

One other version transforms the fine lady:

> 'Ride a cock horse
> To Banbury Cross,
> To see an old woman
> Get up on her horse;
> A ring on her finger,
> A bonnet of straw,
> The strangest old woman
> That ever you saw.'

There is even a French version beginning 'Allons à Dada à Bains-Brie à la croix . . .'. The rhyme has increased the fame of the Cross, yet that has its own legends—for example that the cross goes to drink whenever it hears the church clock strike twelve. Another, invented by J. F. Haynes in the 19th century, is a Gothic fantasy about a jealous knight named Edward, who was betrothed to Matilda of the castle, 'as fair as the rosy morning, as fresh as the sparkling dew, with a face as bright as the starlight night.' He sees her with a strange knight (who, it transpires, is her long lost brother), attacks him, is sorely wounded and nursed back to health by his love. At their marriage she appears at the cross on a white palfrey bedecked with bells.

The present cross was only built in 1859, and does not lie on the site of any of the original three crosses—the High or Market Cross, the Bread Cross and the White Cross.

In 1554 a reference is made to 'the white cross outside the gate called Sugarforde Yate', and in 1606 we hear of 'the great stone called the "White Cross".' It was situated in West Bar Street forming one of the borough boundaries, and may have been destroyed in 1601 with the other crosses, which was why it looked like a stone—or it may have been a stone with a cross painted on it.

The Bread Cross is mentioned in 1648 in a mortgage of property 'in a street called the Sheep Market Street over against the Breadcrosse'. Sheep Market Street was an alternative name for the east end of the High Street, and other sources tell us that the cross stood at the junction of the High Street and Butcher's Row, where butchers and bakers had their stalls. It was built of stone with a slate roof, and was large enough to protect stallholders from the rain.

The main one was the High or Market Cross. Leland describes it in c.1535—'The fayrest strete of the towne lyethe by west and easte down to the river of Charwelle. And at the west parte of this street is a large area invironed with meatlye good buildinge, havynge a goodly crosse withe many degrees about it. In this area is kept every Thursday a very celebrate market.' Beesley interpreted the 'fayrest strete' as the High Street, and the market area as Horsefair, while Potts thought that the large area was the west end of the High Street. However, a 15th century document discovered recently mentions 'the stone cross situated in front of my property on Barkehyll' (an early name for Cornhill), and the present market place has always been the site for the main market. It therefore seems certain that the cross was situated in Cornhill.

Anthony Rivers, a Jesuit priest, wrote about the destruction of the High Cross in 1601; 'The inhabitants of Banbury being far gone in Puritanism, in a furious zeal tumultuously assailed the cross that stood in their marketplace, and so defaced it that they scarcely left one stone upon another. The Bishop of Canterbury thereupon convented the chief actors before him, and by circumstances discovering their riotous proceedings, hath enjoined them

14

to re-edify the same, and bound them over to receive condign punishment before the Lords in the Star Chamber.' It was 1858 before the Archbishop's injunction to rebuild the cross was obeyed!

Matthew Knight had a shop within sight of the cross, and it is his deposition to Star Chamber which gives the most detailed description of the cross and its destruction. It was built of stone, with eight 'grises' or steps around the base on all four sides. The lowest step was 24 feet long each way and two feet broad. A block above the steps formed the base of the shaft, 'a very large and long spire stone', with carvings at the top, including one, or possibly two, crucifixes. On market days people would sit on the steps to display their wares. Matthew Knight explained that the High Cross and the Bread Cross were destroyed by the Puritans because they were venerated by a certain John Trafford of Grimsbury, who would doff his cap as he passed, endangering his immortal soul. The High Cross was destroyed by two masons, who levered up the stones with iron bars, encouraged by William Knight, and when the spire had fallen, Henry Showell smashed the images, crying out 'God be thanked, their god Dagon is fallen down to the ground'.

By 1621 when Bishop Corbet wrote his 'Iter Boreale' he only saw the bases of the crosses:
> 'The crosses also, like old stumps of trees,
> Or stooles for horsemen that have feeble knees,
> Carry no heads above the ground . . .'

The present cross was built in Horsefair in 1858-9 to commemorate the marriage of the Princess Royal, Victoria Adelaide Maria Louise, to Frederick William, Prince of Prussia on January 25 1858. Subscriptions were raised to hold a dress ball, but some people considered that too exclusive. The ball took place, but money was raised for a more permanent memorial—there was great controversy as to whether a cross or a fountain should be built and eventually a compromise was reached by deciding on a cross combined with a conduit. J. Gibbs of Oxford was commissioned to design the monument, and produced a plan for a 'Decorated Gothic' cross with six niches for statues, later amended to three. The foundation stone was laid in April 1859 and although building was stopped temporarily when funds ran out, the cross reached its height of 52 feet and 6 inches in July, when Thomas Ward Boss added the gilt cross at the top. In 1911 statues of King George V, Edward VII and Queen Victoria were added to commemorate King George's coronation.

South Bar about 1850 before the erection of the Cross.

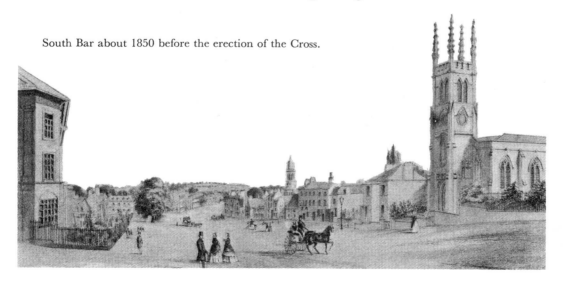

16

ABOVE: The Warwickshire Hunt meets at the Cross.

BELOW: Banbury Cross from the tower of St. Mary's
Church many years ago.

17

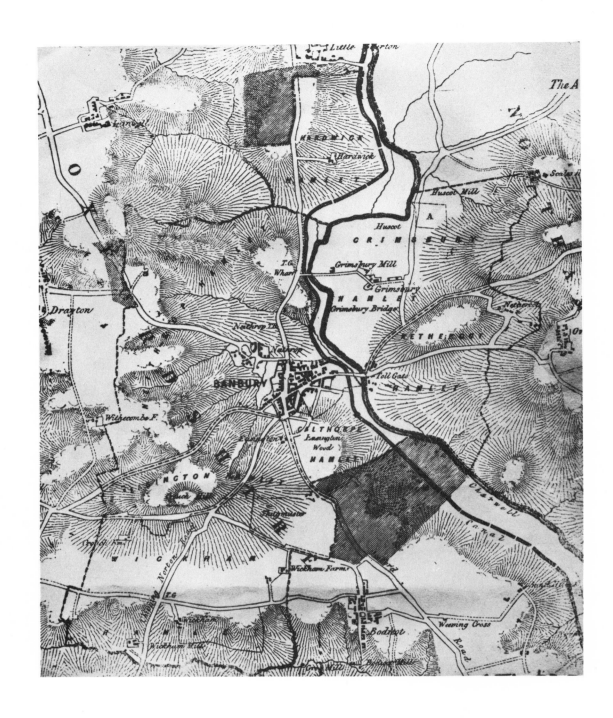

Early Ordnance Survey Map of Banbury (Banbury Museum).

18

Stick, Stock, Stone

Come, butter churn,
Come, butter come,
The great Bull of Banbury
Shan't have none.

'The mosaste parts of the hole towne of Banbyrie standeth in a valley, and is inclosyd by northe and est with low grounde, partly medowes, partly marsche, by southe and southe-west the ground somewhat hillithe in especte of the site of the towne. The fayrest stretch of the towne lyethe by west and easte down to the river of Charwelle.'

Thus John Leland described Banbury when he visited it in the mid 16th century. The area is dominated by red ironstone, which provides fertile farming land and good building material. The location was chosen for settlement because of the good river crossing, and the ancient routes—Banbury Lane and the Jurassic Way, a line of dry ground affording a natural highway in early times and the Salt Way which led to the town from Droitwich.

However, there is no evidence that the area of the town itself was settled before the Anglo Saxon period, although earlier remains have been discovered in the surrounding area. The earliest visitors to the general area were the mesolithic hunters and gatherers who pursued herds of deer across the land bridge from Europe about 12,000 years ago through the forested landscape which developed after the last ice age. They left traces of themselves in their flint tools, which have been picked up in local fields. The first permanent settlement however, began around 6,000 years ago, when groups of neolithic farmers began to clear the woodland and establish farmsteads and fields. Banbury was rather marginal to the main areas of settlement at this time, which were concentrated on the gravel terraces of the Upper Thames valley. Traces of their tombs survive in the 'Whispering Knights' at Rollright, the remains of a megalithic chamber. The spot continued to be venerated, for the circle of the Rollright Stones, built some time around 1600 BC is the remains of a temple or meeting place. Settlement in the region continued to be sporadic. In the late bronze age travelling smiths made axes and swords from imported copper—a lump of copper and a palstave, presumably left by such a smith, were found in Banbury. A sword was lost by a Bronze Age man in what is now South Bar. Most of their burial mounds near Banbury have been ploughed out.

In the Iron Age the territory grew more populous, and the region boasts a large number of hillforts, showing how the landscape was extensively opened up for grazing and farming. The purposes of such forts are varied—they may have been cattle enclosures, as was Tadmarton, defended settlements such as Rainsborough, refuges, estate or tribal centres or have

19

combined several functions. Rainsborough in particular has a complex history. Its massive defences consisted of two ramparts and ditches, an entrance passageway with strong double gates guarded by stone chambers, with a wooden bridge supporting a sentry walk across the top. The site was occupied as early as the sixth century BC, and a century later the fort was built. Once the fort was attacked and burnt; one soldier was trapped in the guardroom and the head of another was left by the battered gateway. The fort was deserted for two centuries, then the ditches were enlarged and new ramparts constructed, but the work was never finished and the fort soon became neglected and deserted.

The Roman settlement was peaceful—the Dobunni, the local Iron Age tribe, welcomed the Romans, who took advantage of the good agricultural land. An extensive settlement was established at Swalcliffe soon after the Romans reached the Cotswolds, with an area of 50 acres, larger than the walled town of Alchester, near Bicester. The wealth of some of the inhabitants is indicated by the number of villas with mosaics. Some of these were designed by artists of the local school of mosaics at Corinium, one of the largest in Europe. The head of Ceres figures on the mosaic of the Thenford villa. The villa there developed from a rectangular agricultural building erected around 320 AD, which was converted for domestic purposes 30 years later, with a porchway, a mosaic lined corridor and three rooms, one of which was heated by a hypocaust. Other rooms were added, including a bath-house. A number of local villas were destroyed by fire, perhaps by the local people when the Romans left or by the marauding Saxons.

The first Saxon settlers reached the Cherwell valley in the 5th century. Settlements were established either side of the ford across the Cherwell—Grimsbury and Banbury. Grim is an alternative name for the god Woden, indicating that it was settled before the area was converted to Christianity. St Birinus came to Wessex in 634, converted King Cynegils, and established his episcopal see in Dorchester, but the area clung tenaciously to paganism for some time after that. 'Bana' is a Saxon personal name and 'bury' an enclosure. Banbury assumed importance as the Bishop of Dorchester's administrative centre for estates which comprised Banbury Hundred. Banbury had a church in Anglo Saxon times and almost certainly a market. Although the town was not granted a market charter until 1155, by 1138-9 it was sufficiently flourishing for the Bishop of Lincoln to be able to grant tolls of £5 a year from its revenue to Godstow Abbey, a substantial sum at that time, indicating that the market was already well established and of long standing. The pre-Conquest settlement was clustered around the church and the churchyard was possibly used as a market place.

Crouch Hill on the outskirts of the town, has a Celtic name and is alleged to have been a pagan religious site—May Day celebrations certainly took place there until quite recently. Legend says that the hill was created by the Devil, who, disguised as a skilled workman, was helping to build Adderbury, Bloxham and Kings Sutton churches. He tripped and accidentally dropped a hod or mortar which became the hill.

Ancient sites have often given rise to folklore and legends, such as those connected with the Rollright Stones. Legend says that a King was marching to war with his army when he met a witch, who told him:

> 'Seven strides thou shalt take,
> And if Long Compton thou can see,
> King of England thou shall be.'

The overjoyed king, confident of success, shouted as he neared the top:

> 'Stick, stock, stone
> As King of England I shall be known.'

Alas, as he took the seventh stride a long earthen barrow arose before him, obscuring the top of the hill, and the witch crowed triumphantly:

> 'As Long Compton thou canst not see
> King of England thou shalt not be,
> Rise up stock, and stand still stone
> For King of England thou shall be none:
> Thou and thy men hoar stones shall be
> And I myself an eldern tree.'

The group of traitorous knights, plotting against the king, were turned into the Whispering Knights and the king became a standing stone. It is said that the stones of the circle can never be accurately counted—a baker was once determined to prove this superstition wrong, and he walked round placing a loaf on each stone as he went round, but he failed to get an accurate total as the fairies stole the loaves. A farmer once wanted to use one of the stones to make a bridge and harnessed a strong team of horses to it, to drag it laboriously down the hill. However, after a number of alarming disturbances the frightened farmer decided to replace the stone, and a single galloping horse was able to haul it back up the hill.

ABOVE: The Rollright Stones.

BELOW: Bronze Age sword found in South Bar (Ashmolean Museum).

ABOVE : Head of Ceres from the Thenford Roman Villa
(Sir Spencer Summers).

BELOW : Mosaic from Wigginton (Beesley).

22

ABOVE: Aerial View of Madmarston Hill fort
(Ashmolean Museum).

BELOW: Shepherd's view of Banbury (Banbury Museum).

23

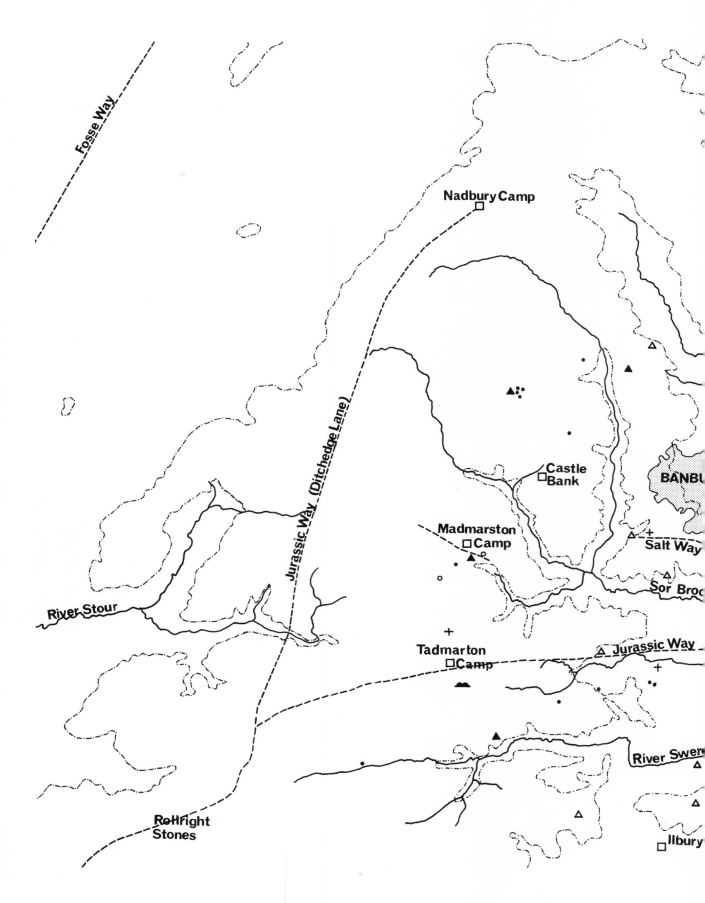

Fosse Way

Nadbury Camp

Jurassic Way (Ditchedge Lane)

BANB

Castle
Bank

Madmarston
Camp

Salt Way

Sor Broo

River Stour

Tadmarton
Camp

Jurassic Way

River Swere

Rollright
Stones

Ilbury

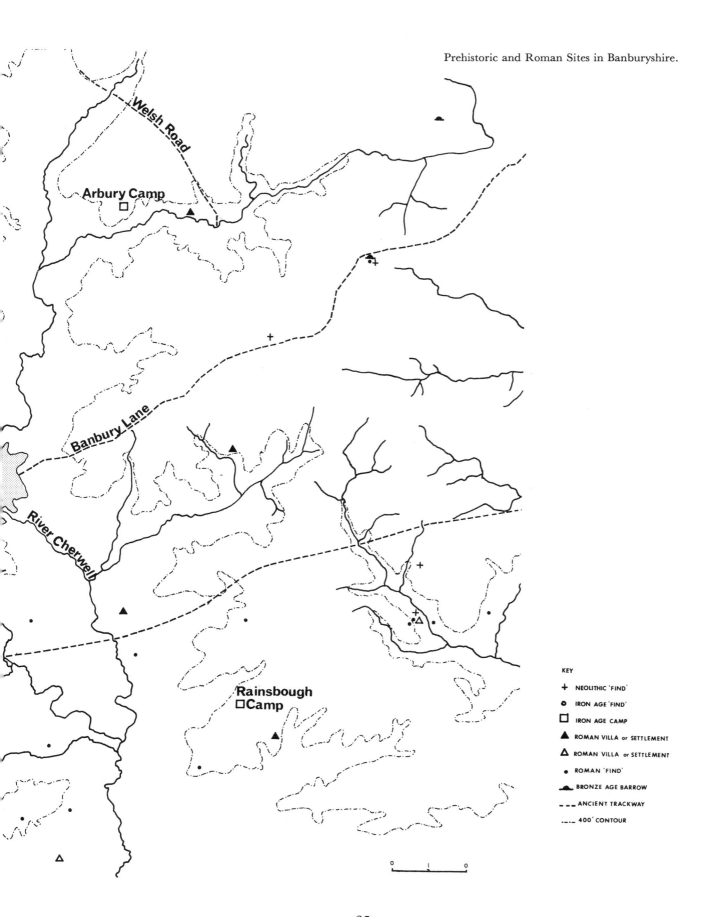

Prehistoric and Roman Sites in Banburyshire.

Welsh Road

Arbury Camp

Banbury Lane

River Cherwell

Rainsbough ▢Camp

KEY

+ NEOLITHIC 'FIND'

● IRON AGE 'FIND'

▢ IRON AGE CAMP

▲ ROMAN VILLA or SETTLEMENT

△ ROMAN VILLA or SETTLEMENT

• ROMAN 'FIND'

▰ BRONZE AGE BARROW

--- ANCIENT TRACKWAY

.--- 400' CONTOUR

0   1   0

ABOVE: Banbury's 13th century bridge.

BELOW: All that can be seen today of Banbury Bridge.

Alexander's Banbury

Sing see-saw, Jack thatching the ridge,
Which is the way to Banbury-bridge.
One foot up and t'other foot down,
And that's the way to Banbury town.

                                    Rusher's Penny Books

Stukeley records an ancient tradition that William the Conqueror once visited Banbury and stayed at the Altarstone Inn. Banbury was then only a large village with a market, and was at first little affected by the Norman Conquest as Ulf, the Saxon Bishop of Dorchester who owned Banbury Hundred, retained his estates. On his death in 1070 they passed to the Norman, Remigius, Bishop of Lincoln, when the see was transferred to Lincoln from Dorchester.

Domesday Book tells us little about the town; Banbury hundred is described as a whole and it is impossible to isolate the town. The hundred included Bourton, Claydon, Wardington, Cropredy, Swalcliffe, Epwell, Shutford, and Fawler (near Charlbury). The entry is as follows:—

'The same Bishop (Lincoln) holdes Banesberie (Banbury). There are fifty hides. Of these the Bishop has in demesne land for ten ploughs and three hides in addition to the inland. The men of the vill (have) 33½ hides. In King Edward's time 33½ ploughs were there and Bishop Remigius found the same number. Now in demesne (there are) 7 ploughs and 14 serfs and 76 villeins with 17 bordars have 33 ploughs. There (are) 3 mills rendering 45 shillings. The pasture has 3 furlongs in length and 2 furlongs in breadth. In King Edward's time it was worth £35; when received £30; now it is worth the same.

Of the land of the manor of Banesberie Robert holds of the Bishop 4 hides; Goisler, 5 hides; the other Robert 2½ hides; William 5 hides, Humphrey ½ hide. There is land for 12½ ploughs. There are 8 ploughs in demesne, and 13 villeins with 3 bordars and 2 serfs have 4 ploughs. There is a mill (belonging to) one of them, Robert the son of Walchelin rendering 5s.4d; and 4 acres of meadow. The whole in King Edward's time was worth £11.10s.; when received £9.10s., now it is worth £14.'

Alexander of Blois the Norman, bishop of Lincoln from 1123-1148, was the real creator of the town of Banbury. William of Malmesbury gives us a description of him; '. . . seeing he was looked upon as a prodigy by reason of his small body, his mind strove to excel and be the more famous in the world.' He enjoyed good living, and was nicknamed 'Alexander the Magnificent'.

Alexander built Banbury Castle, which dominated the town for 500 years; he almost certainly built the Norman church, which, enriched by later additions, was described as 'the cathedral of North Oxfordshire', and he set out the market place and burgage plots between the church and the river.

The castle played an important part in the life of the mediaeval town—the bishops used it as their administrative centre for the region, and it was visited by most mediaeval kings of England. The bishops' military tenants had the duty of castle guard, while a constable administered the castle and part of the bishop's estate. In 1201 the porter was paid 24 shillings, the watchman 15 shillings and the castle ward 10 marks. Leland mentions 'a terrible prison for convict men' in the castle, which was cleaned once a year on Maundy Thursday, when prisoners went into town under guard and collected alms.

The castle was demolished after the Civil War, and there is now no trace to be seen above ground. In 1626 it had two wards, each surrounded by a ditch, with new stone building in the inner ward. Stukeley visited Banbury many years after the castle was demolished but he heard that it had contained lodgings and a chapel. A survey of 1552 gave more details:

'. . . the Castle of Banbury aforesaid, all the houses needful to the same, and the yards and courts; one garden and one orchard, and one parcel of land called the Stewe [fishpond] containing one rood of land, and a certain ditch without the wall of the said Castle, containing 3 acres. . . . Two water mills under one roof lying and being near the Castle. . . . And on a Hame to the same adjoining severally containing 3 acres (a field attached to the mill) . . . one tenement and one garden lying . . . before the gate of the Castle.'

Inquisition 6th Edward VI.

In Elizabeth I's time the castle was in a state of decay and it was estimated that it would cost £50 to repair, and in James I's time we hear of a 23-bay lead-roofed mansion house, and a 6-bay gate house roofed with slate.

Peter Fasham and Kirsty Rodwell have excavated a small part of the site, and concluded that the castle was built in two phases. The original defences consisted of a wide wall set on an earth bank. Much of this was destroyed when the castle was rebuilt about 1300. The second castle was surrounded by two concentric moats filled with water from Cuttle Brook, which flowed down Parson's Street to the Cherwell. A bank was built up between the outer ditch and the 2.2 metre-wide curtain wall which was studded with internal towers. The gate towers were square fronted but may originally have been round. Traces of what could have been a half moon barbican tower have also survived.

In 1547 the castle was purchased by the Duke of Somerset, passing from him to the Duke of Northumberland. It was sold to the crown in 1551 and leased to the Fiennes family of Broughton Castle, who retained it until 1792.

The town was never walled, but there were gateways in archway form at the principal entrances. These were known as 'bars' and three are perpetuated in important street names. The North Bar stood immediately south of the Warwick Road junction. South Bar, known variously as Easington, St. John's and Oxford Bar, stood immediately south of the present St. John's Street—on its demolition about 1785 an obelisk was put up to mark its site, whence the name of Monument Street derived. West Bar (also originally known as Shokersford or Shookewell, later corrupted into Sugarford Bar) was also later known as Bull Bar, after a local inn, and was near the junction with the alley called the Shades. The Cole Bar (probably the same as that referred to occasionally as East Bar) was in Broad Street, which was formerly known as Cole Bar Street. There is no evidence of any gatehouse on the main route from the East, the narrow bridge itself probably being sufficient defence. The bars were all demolished, because of the inconvenience they caused to traffic, at various times in the 18th or early 19th century. Although there were no walls the bars were linked by a lane, parts of which can still be traced in alley ways like the Shades or in actual streets.

The street plan was much the same as today though many street names differed. The bridge across the Cherwell was replaced by a fine stone one in the 13th century, parts of which are still visible today. St. John's Hospital was situated just outside South Bar. It was founded as a hostel for travellers in the early 13th century by Robert Whiting, and the rules were drawn up by Serlo, a prebendary of Banbury. In 1229 the king granted timber from Warwick Gaol to the prior of the hospital so that he could build himself a house. The hospital of St. Leonard, founded about 1265, was situated on the far side of the bridge, outside the town, as a sanctuary for lepers, and is last mentioned in 1391.

About 1285 the borough was extended outside the bars into Newland, which by 1441 had 52 tenements. It seems to have formed a separate entity and had its own traditional customs, such as the Newland Wake, which continued into the 19th century. George Herbert wrote that at the wake the latest comer to the area was elected Mock Mayor and carried shoulder high round Newland, surrounded by his 'officers', with his macebearer carrying an enormous cabbage with its leaves stripped off the stem as his mace. Races were held, the prize being a gaudy waistcoat for the men and a smock or dress length for the women.

Townsmen gradually acquired more of a corporate identity: in 1225, 27 of the town's leading men were selected to make a survey of the town, the 1328 pavage charter of Edward III was headed 'The King to the good man or trustworthy . . .' and in 1337 burgesses went to meet the king in London in connection with raising money for the French wars. A port-moot court, with jurisdiction over the burgage tenants was held in the Hall of Pleas, which probably stood in the market place to judge offences such as selling short weight bread, undersized candles, bad meat, assault and debt. The 2d fine for short-weight bread cannot have been a great deterrent, as one baker was convicted seven times.

The former Banbury Church.

29

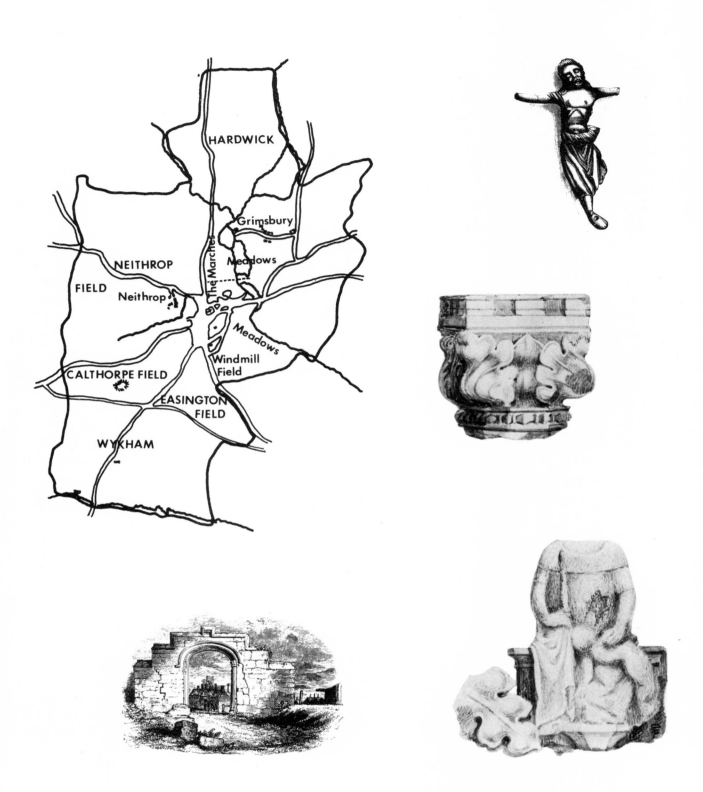

ABOVE LEFT: The settlements of Banbury in medieval times.

ABOVE RIGHT: Bronze crucifix from St John's Hospital (Beesley).

CENTRE AND BELOW RIGHT: Sculptures from St John's Hospital
(Illustrated Beesley, Banbury Library).

BELOW LEFT: St John's Gate (Beesley).

30

LEFT: Alabaster group of the Virgin, Jesus and Joseph, said to be from the chapel of Banbury Castle (Banbury Museum).

ABOVE RIGHT: Bronze medieval spout found in the town, drawn by Jon Hall (Banbury Museum).

BELOW RIGHT: Boar's head found behind the White Hart in Bridge Street (Illustrated Beesley, Banbury Library).

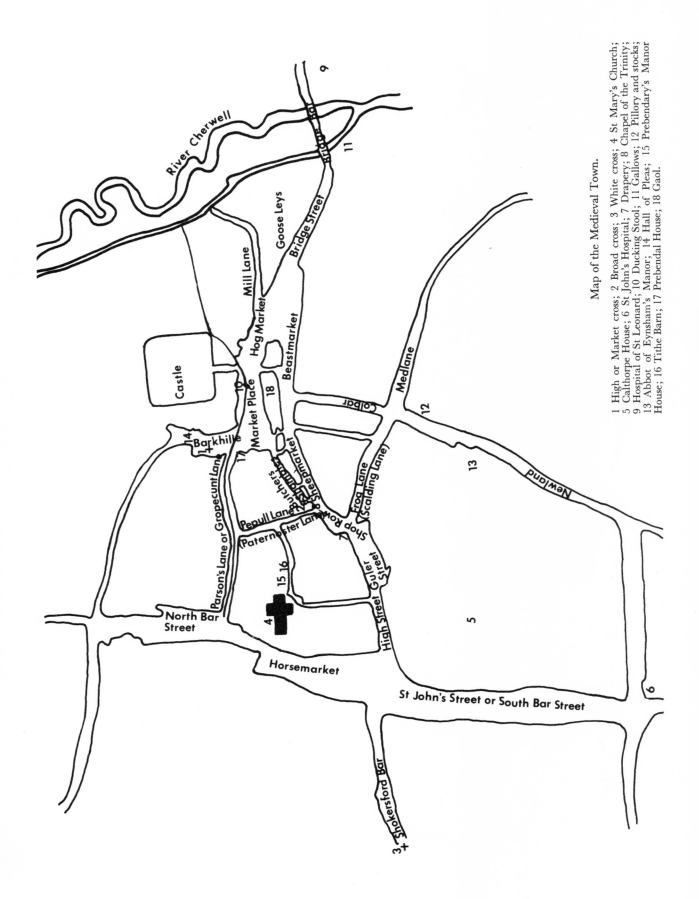

Map of the Medieval Town.

1 High or Market cross; 2 Broad cross; 3 White cross; 4 St Mary's Church; 5 Calthorpe House; 6 St John's Hospital; 7 Drapery; 8 Chapel of the Trinity; 9 Hospital of St Leonard; 10 Ducking Stool; 11 Gallows; 12 Pillory and stocks; 13 Abbot of Eynsham's Manor; 14 Hall of Pleas; 15 Prebendary's Manor House; 16 Tithe Barn; 17 Prebendal House; 18 Gaol.

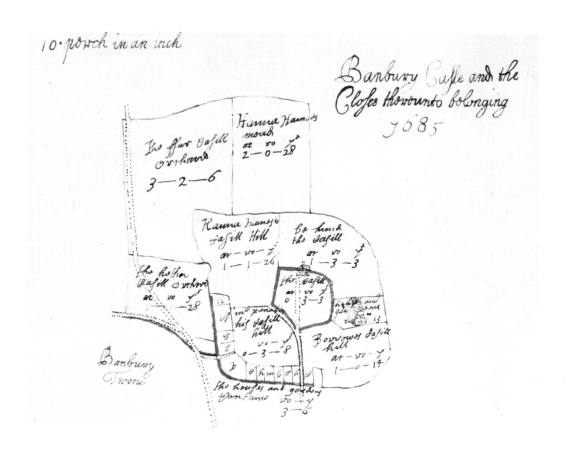

ABOVE: Plan of the site of Banbury Castle (Lord Saye and Sele).

BELOW: Prospect of Banbury from a sketch in the Gough collection (Bodleian Library).

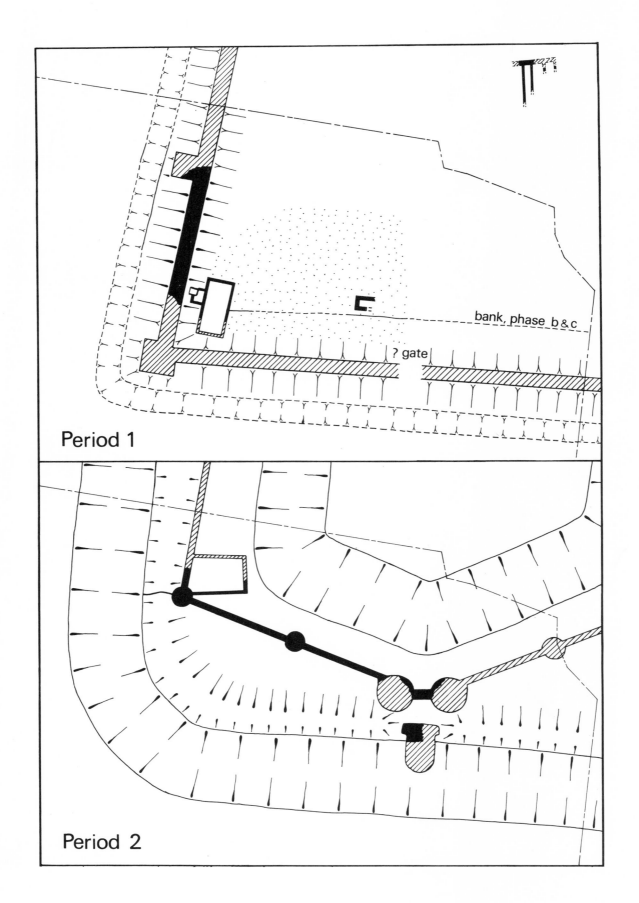

Period 1

Period 2

bank, phase b & c

? gate

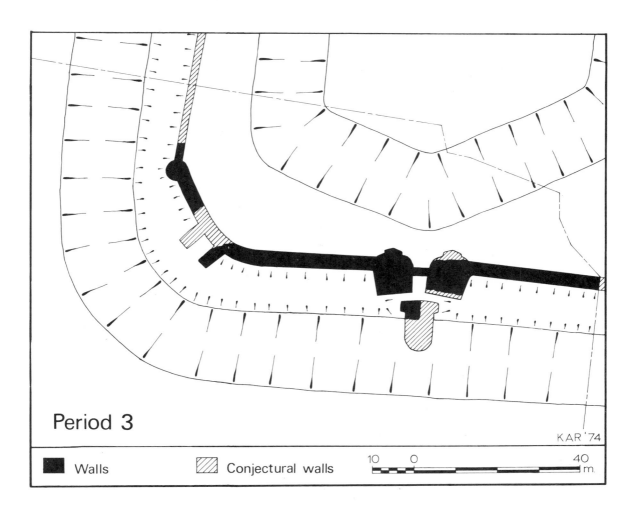

Period 3

KAR '74

■ Walls   ▨ Conjectural walls   10 0   40
                                                              m.

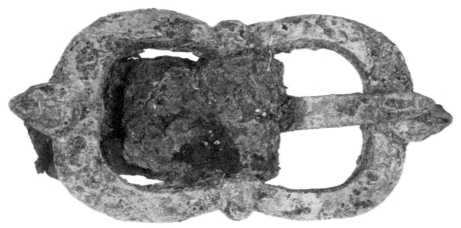

LEFT AND ABOVE: Interpretation of excavations on the site of Banbury
Castle. (Mrs. K. Rodwell, and the Oxfordshire Archaeological Unit).

BELOW: Buckle, from the Castle excavation.

35

S5

S6

S7

S3

50
64

53

door

277

62

96

55

278

279

54

288

56

pitched on edge

28

66

98

36

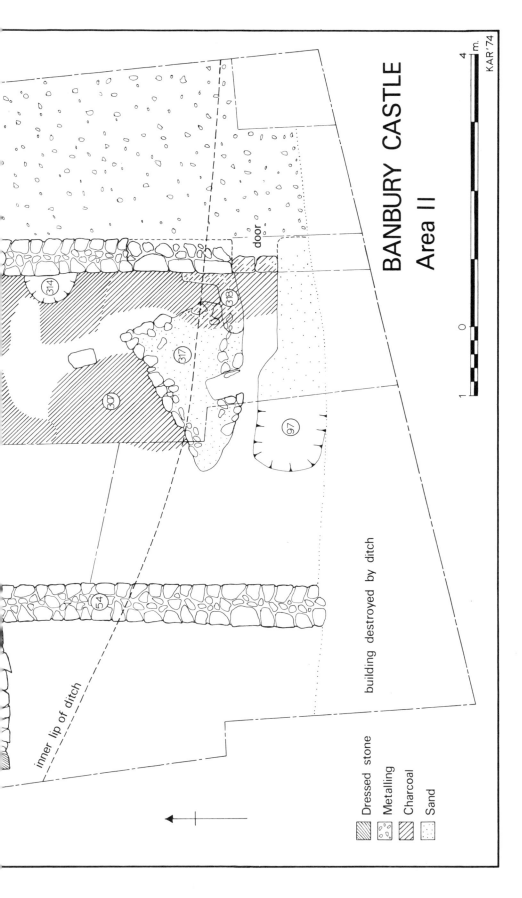

BANBURY CASTLE
Area II

KAR'74

door

inner lip of ditch

building destroyed by ditch

Dressed stone
Metalling
Charcoal
Sand

ABOVE: Castle excavations—further interpretation.
(Mrs. Rodwell and The Archaeological Unit).

37

ABOVE LEFT: Lead scoop.

ABOVE RIGHT: Thimble.

BELOW: 17th century wine bottle (Oxfordshire Archaeological Unit).

(All from the Castle excavations, and on next page).

38

ABOVE LEFT: Silver coin.

ABOVE RIGHT: Spur.

BELOW: Stone slat and window glass.

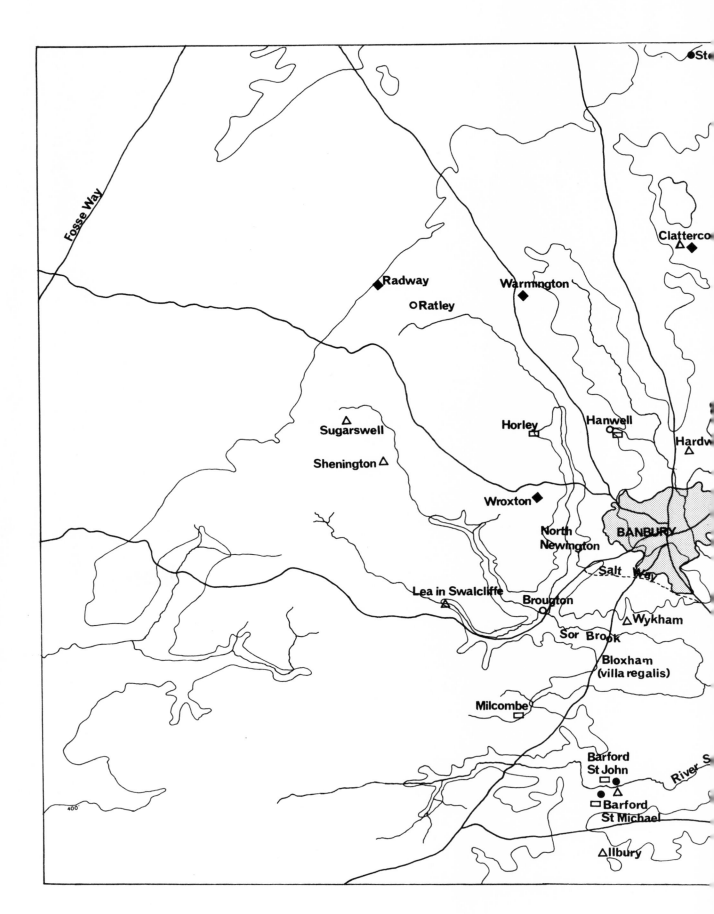

Fosse Way

● Ste

● Radway

○ Ratley

● Warmington

△ ● Clatterco

△ Sugarswell

Shenington △

Horley △
□

Hanwell
○ □

Hardw
△

● Wroxton

North
Newington

BANBURY

Salt Way

Lea in Swalcliffe
△

Broughton
○

Sor Brook

△ Wykham

Bloxham
(villa regalis)

Milcombe
□

Barford
St John
□ ●
● △
□ Barford
St Michael

River S

△ Ilbury

400

40

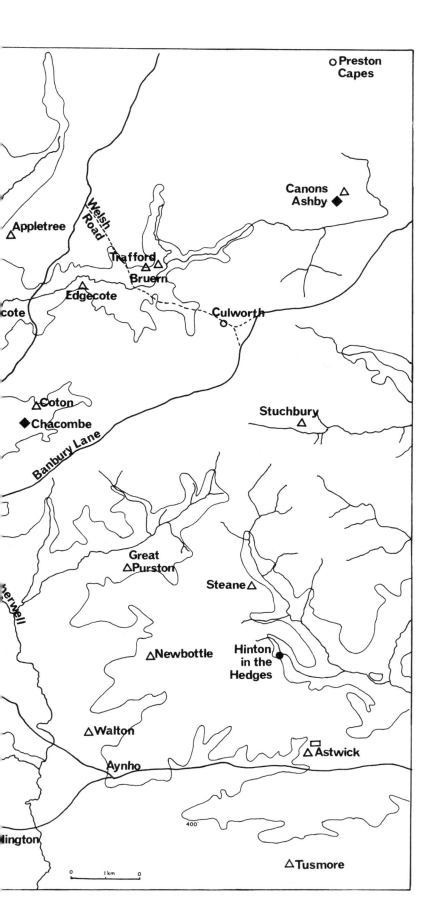

Medieval sites in the Banbury area.

ABOVE LEFT: The Banbury Puritan hanging his cat.

ABOVE RIGHT: Effigy from the church, still in the churchyard (Beesley).

BELOW: The former church (Beesley).

42

Behind the Cross

To Banbury came I, O prophane one!
Where I saw a Puritane one
Hanging of his cat on Monday
For killing of a mouse on Sunday.
(Barnabae Itinerarium by Richard Braithwait 1616).

Banbury has had a church since Saxon times. Alexander, Bishop of Lincoln began the magnificent church here, as befitted the town's position as one of his administrative centres. A local antiquary, Mr Grose, who saw it before its demolition described it as 'an handsome stone edifice having a lofty square Tower crowned with pinnacles and containing six well-tuned bells. This building has something elegant and picturesque in its construction, appearing rather like a Cathedral than a common parochial church.'

An elaborate church did not suit the puritan spirit of the town. As early as 1413 local men took part in the Lollard uprising, and in 1530 Hugh Latimer referred to 'Banbury glosses', indicating the increasingly unorthodox religious views. In 1575 Thomas Brace-bridge, a noted puritan writer and preacher became vicar, to the disgust of the anti-puritan party who eventually deprived him of his living over 'some matters of ceremony'.

William Whateley was one of the most famous puritan divines. His father, twice Mayor of Banbury, had William educated at Christs College Cambridge, where he took his degree in 1604 and was considered 'a good philosopher and a tolerable mathematician'. He was vicar of Banbury from 1610 until his death thirty years later. His vociferous preaching earned him the nickname of 'the roaring boy'—he gave a terrifying sermon, 'Sinne no More', after the Great Fire which destroyed a third of the town in 1628, blaming it all on the sins of the people. One of his publications, 'The Bride Bush' promulgated the view that adultery or a long desertion dissolved a marriage, but he had to withdraw this view when challenged by the High Commission Court.

By the early 17th century the very name of Banbury was synonymous with Puritanism—and in 1610 the English version of Camden's 'Britannia' referred to it as a town noted for 'cheese, cakes and zeal', and many playwrights made Banbury a butt for their jokes, such as William Davenant in 'The Wits' (1636):

> 'Here dwells a lady
> That hath not seen a street since good King Harry
> Call'd her to a mask; she is more devout
> That a weaver of Banbury, that hopes
> To intice Heaven, by singing, to make him lord of twenty looms.'

One of the 17th century churchwardens, Sharp was so stimulated by a sermon on the

43

theme 'that it is the duty of every Christian to put his hand to the pulling down of idolatry' that he proceeded to destroy many images in the church. It was further damaged during the Civil War, when it was occupied by troops and served as a battery for firing on the castle.

Such depredations made the church unsafe. Ugly buttresses were erected to hold up the west end, but much of the sculpture and armorial glass had been destroyed and the interior marred by the construction of a Georgian gallery and box pews. Several reports on the fabric were made and in 1790 Samuel Pepys Cockerell agreed that it was dangerous and was commissioned to design the new church. An Act of Parliament was passed to raise money for the new building, by which anyone who subscribed £50 could become a Trustee, up to £6,000 could be borrowed and a rate of 3/6d in the £ levied for building work. Money was raised by selling lead, stone, 'an Altar Piece of good English Oak, with four marble Tables on which are inscribed the Lord's Prayer, Ten Commandments and the Belief . . . also the Rails and Communion Table in exceeding good order having been lately repaired; an excellent good painting of the King's Arms in Oil on Canvas, in a Frame of Wood painted and gilt; a considerable quantity of large Doors of Various Dimensions . . . part perfectly well adapted for Coach Houses.'

The Church began to collapse the day before demolition commenced—the aisle fell in and the Gentleman's Magazine reported that 'the crash was heard near two miles from the spot. On the following day the Tower likewise fell. The arches on which it stood first gave way, which occasioned the chasm from the bottom to the top, and instantly the whole tower became cracked and shivered in a variety of directions, admitting the light through each, but yet preserving a perpendicular fall, even its pinnacles.'

Ten horses were harnessed to the buttressed west end to pull it down but the spring of the wall was so great that some of them were pulled up into the air; gunpowder was used to demolish stubborn remnants of fabric. Although the Act had made provision for the monuments in the old church to be carefully removed and put in the new one, at the expense of families concerned, few bothered.

Stone was quarried from Adderbury, Bretch Hill and Burton Dassett, and the Attleborough stone for the columns of the nave was brought down the newly opened Oxford Canal.

Pews were a status symbol and sums of £100 and £50 were subscribed for them, raising £5,000. On September 15, 1797 the church was consecrated, though the tower, designed by S. P. Cockerell's son Robert, was not built until 1820, owing to shortage of funds, leading to the taunt:

> 'Dirty Banbury's proud people
> Built a church without a steeple.'

In 1654 John and Anne Audland, noted Quakers preached so vehemently in the town that Anne was put in Banbury gaol. She converted Edward Vivers who purchased land for the Friends Meeting House. A replacement building on the same site (the north-western corner of the Horsefair), and still in use, since 1790 has been the oldest place of worship in the town.

In 1860 Banbury was visited by the methodist revival preachers, Dr Palmer and his wife Phoebe, as part of their campaign to convert the children of the religious. At least one Banburian, William Bunton, was unimpressed:

'If instead of assisting in these mischievous revivals, ... I say mischievous, for where they do not entirely destroy the reason they prostrate the soul, upset the mind and render their victims unfit for the business of life . . . would they but use their efforts in a sober and useful purpose, much good would result from their labours and happiness be achieved.'

The Baptist movement flourished. When it started in Banbury in 1737, the town was considered to be in 'deplorable darkness'. The congregation in the chapel opened in Church Passage in 1792 had Calvinistic views. The Chapel opened in Bridge Street in 1841 was inspired by a leading local baptist, Caleb Clarke. He was a man with 'almost supernatural' gifts for medicine, who gave up his hosiery business in 1850 to devote himself to medicine, armed with a purchased German diploma and a licence to sell patent medicines. In his first year he attracted 12,000 patients. Despite his eloquent preaching, he was not made pastor of the church, to his great disappointment, perhaps because the multitudes who attended his services frightened away the middle classes. The Austin family of brewing fame patronised the congregation in South Bar from 1834-52, while the West Bar chapel which flourished from 1829-77 was the property of the Gardner ironmongery family.

Half the population of the town in the mid 19th century was non-conformist. The protest against the primacy of the Church of England was linked with the attack on the aristocratic domination of the town. Banbury was a pocket borough from the late 17th century until the Reform Act of 1836, under the influence of the North family who lived at nearby Wroxton Abbey.

With reform, the non-Anglican representation on the council increased, and they proved their power in 1836 by abolishing the Mayor's Sunday morning church parade. The Wesleyans attracted a wide spectrum of the population from the poorer to the business and professional classes, while Presbyterians and Unitarians tended to be traders. Anti-Catholic feeling was strong—there had been few recusants and when St. John's, the new Catholic Church was consecrated in 1838 a pamphlet was issued entitled 'The Abominations of Popery Displayed'.

LEFT: William Whately (Beesley).

RIGHT: The vicarage before its Victorian alterations.

ABOVE LEFT: Presbyterian meeting house.

CENTRE RIGHT: Baptist chapel, Bridge Street.

CENTRE LEFT: Austin House, a Calvinistic Chapel
built by Richard Austin in 1834.

CENTRE BELOW: St. John's Catholic Church.

BELOW RIGHT: Statuary from the old church (Beesley).

ABOVE RIGHT: Frontispiece of a sermon preached by Whately on the
occasion of the great fire in the town (Banbury Library).

46

ABOVE LEFT : The Methodist church hall.

ABOVE RIGHT : The Friends' Meeting House in Horsefair,
Banbury's earliest remaining place of worship.

BELOW RIGHT : Congregational church, South Bar.

CENTRE LEFT : The Baptist chapel as it appears today—
amalgamated into Fine Fare.

BELOW LEFT : New Baptist chapel, Horsefair.

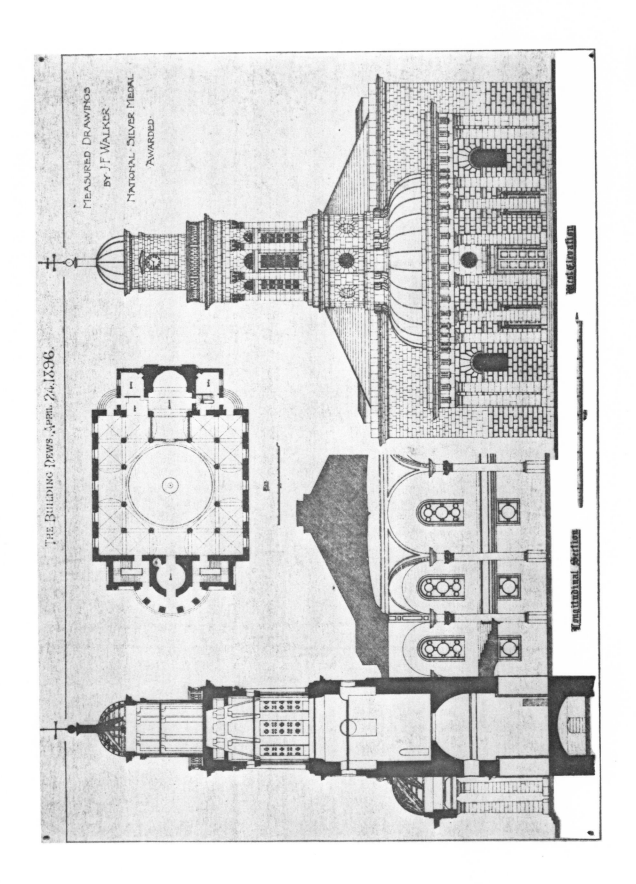

Plan and elevation of the new church.

St Mary's church, drawn by John Bloxham.

THE HON.BLE COLONEL
NATHANIEL FINES.
MIREVELT. PINXᵗ

Nathaniel Fiennes (Lord Saye and Sele).

50

Civil Commotion

On the seventh day on the seventh month most lamentablye
The men of Babylon did spoyle the tribe of Banburye.
Then were called up our men of warr, young Vivers, Cooke and Denys,
Whom our lord Sea placed under his son Master ffenys.

Banbury was a relatively peaceful town during the middle ages, though it was briefly affected by the Wars of the Roses in 1469. Insurgent Lancastrians marched south and were met by the royalist army under the Earl of Pembroke and the Earl of Devon. Pembroke had 7-8,000 men and Devon 4-5,000 men and a quarrel broke out about quartering their men in Banbury, which led to the withdrawal of Devon. Because of this the royalists were defeated at Danes Moor, near Edgcott and tradition has it that the Earl of Pembroke and eleven others were beheaded in the porch of Banbury church.

Banbury's Puritanism led it to support the Parliamentarians in the Civil War; in 1627 there was opposition to the King's forced loan; in 1628 Lord Saye and Sele was behind the problems over quartering troops in the town, and Banbury men showed a great reluctance to pay Ship Money.

William Fiennes, Lord Saye and Sele, and his second son Nathaniel, the MP for Banbury, were strong Puritans and they had great influence locally, though Spencer Compton, Earl of Northampton, who lived at Compton Wynyates, rallied people to the royalist cause. In July 1642, even before the king had raised his standard at Nottingham, there was confrontation over six pieces of ordnance held in Banbury Castle, claimed by Lord Brooke, the parliamentarian, and by Spencer Compton, who forced the garrison to surrender them to him.

The first major battle of the war was fought on October 23, 1642 at Edgehill only a few miles from Banbury. Neither side had had time to get properly organised—the foot regiments on both sides were wearing red jackets, and discipline was poor. The king set out from Shrewsbury to march to London, quartering each night in villages. The Royalists took ten days to arrive in the neighbourhood of Banbury as the army was slow and unwieldy. Essex, who led the Parliamentarian forces, met the Prince of Wales at Wormleighton, north of Banbury and some Roundheads were captured. The Royalists established themselves on the slope at Edgehill, assembling before dawn, with the Parliamentarians near the bottom of the hill. After a preliminary bombardment the Royalists advanced. Both wings of cavalry routed their opponents and they chased them for two miles, headed by Prince Rupert, but they lost their advantage by wasting time plundering the baggage train. The foot regiments on both sides fought closely and two of the five Royalist brigades were broken and about 1,500 men killed. Both sides were completely exhausted by the end of the day, and neither

51

relished the thought of continuing the fight the next day. Essex marched away with his men, leaving the King a token victory, whereas if he had routed the Parliamentarians he could have ended the Civil War.

Perhaps because this was the first battle of the war, it was followed by the sighting of apparitions. Two pamphlets were published, saying that in Kineton, near the scene of the battle, were heard 'fearfull and strange apparitions of spirits as sounds of drums, trumpets, with the discharging of Canons Muskies, Carbines pettronels, to the terrour and amazement, of all the fearfull hearers and behoulders'; shepherds and countrymen heard 'the sounds of drums afar off, and the noise of soldiers as it were giving out their last groans', and saw a troop of horse arriving at full speed and then sinking into the earth. Some corpses were found unburied, and after their burial, apparitions ceased, although people claimed to have seen them in the 1860s and in 1960.

Three days later Banbury castle surrendered to the King, and half its garrison took service under him. The castle was held for the king under the command of various members of the Compton family for the next three and a half years. Several hundred troops were quartered in the castle and some in the town, Banbury forming a royalist stronghold in a predominantly Parliamentarian area. Forays were made to intercept troops and obtain supplies and money so that Banbury could supply the royalist forces at Oxford. Roundheads unsuccessfully attempted to take the town in December 1642 and May 1643. A skirmish took place in 1643 at Middleton Cheney, where the Roundheads were totally defeated. (Cromwell visited Banbury briefly in 1644, driving the Cavaliers into the Castle). The next major battle in the area was that of Cropredy Bridge in 1644, the culmination of the year's manoeuvres, during which the King escaped from beleaguered Oxford, to campaign in the Midlands. His opponents, Essex and Waller, divided their forces, which together far outnumbered the King's, and Charles gathered his army together at Witney to attack Waller in June 1644, before heading for Daventry, but hearing that Waller was near Banbury changed his plans. His army stopped for the night east of Banbury, with Waller at Hanwell. Both armies manoeuvred for Crouch Hill, which Waller reached first and that afternoon there were a few skirmishes. The King slept the night at a yeoman's house in Grimsbury.

Waller drew his army up on Bourton Hill, and a party of Royalists guarded Cropredy Bridge, a narrow packhorse bridge over the Cherwell, north of Banbury. As there was about a mile and a half gap between the front and rear of the King's army, Waller decided to rush the two river crossings of the Cherwell with two detachments of horse—the battle commenced at about one o'clock, but the Roundheads were badly informed about the whereabouts of the Royalist army and instead of cutting off the King's rear as they had intended, they were trapped between two fires.

After a confusing battle the Royalists captured the ford and the mill, but failed to take the bridge. The King wanted to avoid further bloodshed and sent a message to Waller that if the officers and soldiers laid down their arms they would be pardoned, to which Waller replied that the King would have to address himself to Parliament. The armies both stood in the same positions the next day, to see who would quit the field first; the news that Round-head support was at Buckingham caused the King to march to Evesham leaving Waller defeated and broken in spirit, ending a campaign which favoured the Royalists.

As the King's army moved further away, the Roundheads decided to try to recapture Banbury Castle. They spent July 1644 constructing siegeworks in the Market Place and North Bar destroying houses near the castle and setting up batteries, including putting guns in the church tower. Reinforcements arrived in September. On September 5 the royalist newsheet reported:

'This morning we were certified that the rebels planted without the North Gate of the Towne near Nethorpe; from whence they played with their cannon all yesterday and Tuesday; in which time they shot 80 granadoes of 112 lb weight, and 160 canon shot, the least 18 lb, and the biggest 32 lb bullet, against the West part of the Castle. . . . The garrison souldiers are exceeding hearty, much heightned by the exemplary courage of that valiant young knight Sir William Compton, brother to the Earle of Northampton'.

Mercurius Aulicus 1644 pp 1146-47.

The Roundheads made an unsuccessful attempt to storm the castle on September 23 and at the end of the month enlisted the aid of Jacob Keilenbury, the parliamentary chief engineer. Several unsuccessful attempts were made by local royalists to raise the siege, which was finally abandoned by the parliamentarians when news was heard on October 25, of the approach of a Royalist army under the Earl of Northampton.

The castle defences were strengthened after the siege—100 men were employed in digging a new moat and by 1645 two new bulwarks and two sally ports were completed. Many buildings in the Market Place area had to be demolished to leave space between town and castle. Three hundred men repaired a length of wall which fell down during extensions.

The castle was again beseiged in 1646. Much of the cavalry had left the garrison to join the King, so it was undermanned when the siege was started in January by Edward Whalley with 3,000 men. Nineteen-year-old Sir William Compton commanded the castle with only 300 men. In May, further mortars and heavy guns were acquired by the Roundheads and on the 8th, after fifteen weeks the Castle surrendered, probably because of incursions by the Parliamentarian siegeworks and news of the King's flight to Scotland. They found in the Castle; '500 musquets . . ., many pikes and other armes, nine colours, 10 pieces of ordnance, 12 barrels of powder, almost a tun of match, good store of byllets' (Moderate Intelligencer No. 62).

The Civil War had little more impact on the town. In 1646 the castle's defences were destroyed, and the castle returned to Lord Saye and Sele, but the townsfolk petitioned for its demolition so that materials could be used to repair the battered town. It was purchased for £2,000 and pulled down, leaving two small buildings which Lord Saye and Sele had recently built for the Hundred Courts. In 1712 all that could be seen was 'the remains of four bastions, a brook running without them' (Stukeley).

The peace of the town was again disrupted in 1800 as food riots took place throughout the country. Many voters came from outside Banbury, including stocking weavers from Middleton Cheney and colliers from Warwickshire. During the first riot on September 11 there was 'partial mischief amongst the butter people', when the Red Lion was attacked and food was sold at reduced prices. Horse troops were called in, who charged the mob on September 15—a child was killed.

In 1830 Banbury was involved in the 'Swing' riots; agricultural labourers in the villages of Kings Sutton, Tadmarton and Upper Boddington began destroying thrashing machines, but in Banbury it was mainly small craftsmen and tradesmen who were involved in riots possibly because of dissatisfaction about high rates and taxation. George Herbert said it was started by boys who collected in North Bar; they decided to set fire to the threshing machines at Joey Pain's farm in Neithrop. The noise of the fire bells attracted local inhabitants to the fire. The Mayor swore in as many people as he could find as special constables; Thomas Cobb's Yeomanry were called out:

'They marched down towards the fire where the people were all congregated and orders were given to disperse them which they partially did, but some of the crowd seized hold of the long cross bars which were used for attaching the horses to the threshing machine and were, I should think, about 20 foot long and by this time were all ablaze. They rushed at the Yeomanry horses, and swang them amongst them. This so frightened the horses that they lost all command of them.'

The Yeomanry then spread the rumour that they were about to fire on the crowd, and marched towards them with drawn swords to which the rabble retaliated by collecting stones in their smock-frocks and throwing them, causing the Yeomanry to retreat. The special constables finally dispersed the crowd and about 20 people were brought to trial. Dragoons put a stop to disturbances the next day in neighbouring parishes. The riots probably hastened wage rises.

ABOVE: The Battle of Edgehill (Banbury Museum).

BELOW LEFT: Cannon and Market balls.

BELOW RIGHT: Spencer Compton, Earl of
Northampton (Banbury Library)

ABOVE LEFT: Prince Rupert (Banbury Library).

ABOVE RIGHT: The Earl of Essex (Banbury Library).

BELOW RIGHT: Sir William Compton (J. S. W. Gibson).

BELOW LEFT: 'When did you last see your father?' A trial said to have taken place in the Globe Room of the Reindeer Inn.

55

Part of the map from Dr Plot's History of Oxfordshire 1677.

INSET RIGHT: King Charles I.

INSET LEFT: Civil War helmet (Lord Saye and Sele).

ABOVE LEFT: Miniature of a second lieutenant of the
Banbury Military Association *c.* 1800.

ABOVE RIGHT: Banbury Gas Works after it received a direct hit from
the only bomb to hit Banbury during World War II.

BELOW: The war memorial in the People's Park commemorating the 325
men and one woman who gave their lives for their country in the 1914-18
War and those who fell in the 1939-45 War.

Manners Makyth Man

Ride a cock horse to Banbury Cross
To see a Fiennes Lady on a White Horse
With rings on her fingers and bells on her toes.

Banbury's past has been influenced by a number of prominent families—the Fiennes and their descendants at Broughton, the Copes of Hanwell, the Danvers and Dashwoods of Calthorpe, the Comptons of Compton Wynyates and the Norths of Wroxton.

In 1392 Broughton Castle was purchased by William of Wykeham, Bishop of Winchester, and Edward II's Chancellor, after the male line of the de Broughtons had died out. William was the founder of Winchester College and New College, Oxford, and in his will he stated that his descendants should be allowed free entrance to Winchester. Broughton Castle descended to the Fiennes family—William Fiennes, 1st Viscount Saye and Sele, was born in 1582 and educated at Winchester and New College. He had a strong belief in heredity and the constitutional rights of the House of Lords, and he ardently supported parliamentary rights against the arbitrary government of Charles I. He was a strong puritan, the 'god-father' of the Puritan party. He gathered at Broughton many leaders of the Puritan party—Hampden, Pym, St. John, Lord Brooke, Lord Holland, Vane, the Earls of Bedford, Warwick and Essex, and his own son Nathaniel—who consulted in his Council Chamber. His nickname was 'Old Subtlety', and his contemporary, Clarendon, the Civil War historian, described him as 'a man who had the deepest hand in the original contrivance of all the calamities which befell this unhappy kingdom'. When the civil war broke out he raised a regiment for Parliament to fight at the battle of Edgehill, and his sons, John and Nathaniel, both fought in the Parliamentary army. Despite his encouragement of the Parliamentarians he refused to have anything to do with the execution of Charles I and discouraged other peers from doing so. He retired to Lundy after the king's execution, and welcomed the restoration of Charles II. He was involved in the colonial venture of the puritan Providence Company, which tried to build a puritan community on islands near Nicaragua, to which he subscribed £4,000, and also contributed to Saybrook in Connecticutt.

Broughton Castle has remained in the Fiennes and Twistleton families to the present day —in 1847 Frederick Benjamin Twistleton acknowledged his debt to his ancestors by adding 'Wykeham—Fiennes' to his surname; through Margaret Wykeham her husband William Fiennes came to Broughton in the 15th century and in the 18th, Elizabeth Fiennes left Broughton to her grandson Fiennes Twistleton.

The rivals of the Fiennes family during the Civil War were the Comptons of Compton Wynyates. Spencer Compton, Earl of Northampton, raised a regiment for the Royalists and his nineteen year old son William gallantly defended Banbury Castle. When he was challenged to deliver the castle to his besiegers he wrote:

'I shall never be so false to my king as to deliver up the trust I have from him to Rebels; I shall therefore desire you to forbeare any further frivolous summons; for I thanke God, I have a loyall hart, as I shall make you sensible of in defence of this place (by God's assistance) if you make any further attempts upon it. All the Officers and Soldiers now here with me, returne the same resolutions, rather choosing to lose our lives in the defence of this place than deliver it up without his Majestie's command; I rest yours in what I may
W. Compton   Banbury Castle the 18th of March 1645.'

Several prominent families have owned Calthorpe House, which was built in the mid 16th century for George Danvers. His son John was violently opposed to puritanism, which brought him into conflict with Anthony Cope of Hanwell, MP for Banbury. Cope was well known for his puritan views and braved the ire of Elizabeth I by introducing a new Book of Common Prayer into the House of Commons, when the Queen had expressly told her parliament not to meddle in matters of religion. He won a spell in the Tower of London for his pains. In Banbury, Cope attacked maypoles, particularly the one in Neithrop, as being ungodly. In 1589 he ordered William Long, Constable of Neithrop and Calthorpe, to suppress all local Whitsun Ales, May games and morris dances. John Danvers was sheriff of Oxford, and he persuaded the council that such amusements should be permitted. The Oxford Assizes reversed this decision, so Danvers left the area, leaving Anthony Cope supreme. Cope was influential locally, and twice entertained James I.

Calthorpe House was sold to the Hawtayne family—Harry Hawtayne's mother was the daughter of Lawrence Washington of Sulgrave, ancestor of the American President, George Washington. The Dashwood family owned Calthorpe for a time but never lived there, and in the late 18th century the house was leased to the Cobb family and used as a wool manufactory. Sir Robert Dashwood, MP for Banbury in the late 18th century lived at Wickham Park—his house is now Tudor Hall Girls School.

The present Wroxton Abbey was built by Sir William Pope around 1615 and visited soon after by James I. Through his marriage to Lady Frances Pope, Sir Francis North inherited Wroxton in 1681, when he bought out the shares her sisters had in the manor. His family continued to lease the manors and rectories from Trinity until the male line died out in 1827. Colonel J. S. Doyle who married Susan, granddaughter of the Earl of Guilford, changed his name to North, so the family maintained its connection with Wroxton until 1932. Sir Dudley North, who became Tory MP for the borough of Banbury in 1685 was the first of seven members of the North family to represent the town between 1685 and 1818. The Norths made liberal gifts to the town: in 1711 they rebuilt the almshouses, they donated a bell to the rebuilt church in 1820, endowed the Blue Coat school and were trustees for Sprigge's charity. They exercised considerable influence over the corporation, affording government patronage to local people.

Banbury had a noted MP in Frederick, Lord North. In 1754, at the age of 22 he was elected and in 1770 he became First Lord of the Treasury and held the office of Prime Minister for 12 years. It was during his premiership that the American colonies gained their independence.

In 1827 Wroxton was inherited by John, Marquess of Bute, through his marriage to the daughter of George Augustus, Earl of Guilford, but he did not live at Wroxton and took no personal influence in Banbury, so North influence waned.

ABOVE LEFT: William Fiennes, 1st Viscount Saye and Sele.

ABOVE RIGHT: Grant of the castle by Elizabeth I to Richard Fiennes
in 1595 (Lord Saye and Sele).

BELOW: Broughton Castle.

61

ABOVE: The Appointment of William, Lord Saye and Sele, as Lord High
Steward of Banbury in 1632 by Charles I. (Lord Saye and Sele).

BELOW: Deed of Appointment by Charles I, of Lord Saye and
Sele as Master of the Court of Wards in 1642.

ABOVE: The great hall, Broughton Castle.

BELOW LEFT: Sir Robert Dashwood (Banbury Museum).

BELOW RIGHT: Hanwell gatehouse.

ABOVE: Calthorpe House.

BELOW: Armorial glass from Calthorpe House.

LEFT: The arms of the Danvers family.

CENTRE: The arms of the Doyley family.

RIGHT: The arms of Danvers and Doyley family (Banbury Museum).

ABOVE: Drawing of Wroxton Abbey in 1781.
BELOW: Compton Wynyates (J. S. W. Gibson).

65

BOROUGH OF BANBURY.

NOTICE

FOR THE BETTER REGULATION OF THE

MARKETS & FAIRS.

I HEREBY GIVE NOTICE, that on and after Thursday, the 30th day of September instant, all

CATTLE,

SHEEP, AND PIGS

Brought to the Markets and Fairs of this Borough must be removed from the Market or Fair by four o'clock in the afternoon.

AND I HEREBY require the Owner or person having charge of such Cattle, Sheep, or Pigs to remove the same accordingly.

Joseph Osborn,

Mayor and Clerk of the Market.

Banbury, 13th September, 1869.

CHENEY, PRINTER, BANBURY

Victorian market poster.

Mop Fairs and Markets

As I was going to Banbury,
Upon a summer's day,
My dame had butter, eggs and fruit
And I had corn and hay.
Joe drove the ox, and Tom the swine,
Dick took the foal and mare,
I sold them all—then home to dine,
From famous Banbury fair.

Fairs and markets have always played an important part in the town. A market existed in Banbury in Anglo-Saxon times, and in 1155 Henry II granted Banbury the right of holding a market every Thursday. By 1154 there was an annual fair in Whit Week. Queen Mary confirmed the Thursday market in the town's charter of 1554, which also granted two fairs a year.

Mediaeval street names indicate that the market was divided into areas—the Ox Market (recorded in 1319), the Sheep Market (1441), Horse Market (1552) and Cornmarket (1606). People living in Sheep Street were entitled to erect sheep pens there on market days and charge for their use. The general market was held in the market place. Leland visiting Banbury in the reign of Henry VIII wrote that 'there was kept every Thursday a very celebrate market'. Gradually certain market days became associated with particular products. Fish fair day in 1555 was Thursday February 28, Leather fair day in 1558 was Thursday January 3, and in 1606 the name 'Horse Market' was changed to 'Horse Fair'.

Dr Plot mentions a 'Mop Fair' in 1677—a hiring fair, where servants wore badges to indicate their skills. Mop fairs continued into the 20th century, as part of the Michaelmas Fair and were great social occasions. Thomas Ward Boss described a fair of about 1850:

'The greater part of the domestic servants only left their place once a year, and this was therefore their only holiday of the year . . . all stood in the streets in groups, seeking new masters and mistresses; the farmers seeking grooms, waggoners, and shepherds, who stood waiting to be hired. Some had bunches of whipcord, horse hair or wool in their button-holes, which represented their respective callings. . . . Hiring was a busy feature for several hours during the Fair—the normal time for the hiring contract being one year, the payment of one shilling over to the servant being the seal of engagement.'

But by 1856 the statute fair was declining and most of the servants looking for hire were girls of twelve to fifteen years.

The Great Western Railway ran two cheap excursion trains which brought about 1,000 from the stations between here and Wolverhampton and more from Abingdon, Oxford and intermediate stations. Obviously it was a great attraction to people from miles around:

'Early on Tuesday morning, Market Place, Cornhill and Bridge Street, much resembled a hive of bees; a vast multitude laboured with all their might in fastening together boarding and canvas. . . . Large parties of visitors came from all the towns and villages around in carts, vans and all kinds of carriages, and on foot. The fair was literally packed with human bodies. There was an extraordinary attendance of over-grown boys and girls, women and children of all ages, who flocked into town by all manner of means. They bought ribbons and shawls, dolls and toys, ate gingerbread and Banbury cake.'
(1856 eye witness report, reprinted in Banbury Guardian on October 13, 1966).

Today it is largely a pleasure fair but even in the 19th century entertainment was far more varied. In 1856 there were two menageries, three theatrical companies, boxing booths; organs played in the streets, groups of tumblers performed, Punch and Judy appeared, ballad singers sang love themes; peep shows alone showed that England was at war with Russia—one was 'Scenes in the Russian War', and another portrayed 'Trial and Execution of Dr Palmer, the notorious poisoner'. 'A member of Burton's Dramatic Establishment feigned the agonies of hanging by the neck' (Banbury Guardian). Side shows included shooting galleries, photographic booths, aerial boats, hobby horses, wheels of fortune and 'a long row of stalls selling everything from a needle to Banbury cakes and ready made clothes'.

The business fair was an important element. In 1856 81 trucks of cattle were despatched by train, eight horses were sold in Horsefair at prices between £11 and £18.10s; 12 steers were auctioned in Cow Fair at an average of £15.15s each. Sheep dealing is mentioned in Banbury in the 19th century. The Buckett brothers used to buy fat sheep at fairs and markets and send them to London. Banbury was on a major drove road from Wales to London, and animals were often driven through the town; 'A great number of cattle from Wales and Herefordshire used to trek through Banbury to Northampton and the grazing lands of the Eastern Counties. I have known as many as 2,000 pass through Banbury in a day; they would not travel more than two miles per hour. Large herds of fat cattle would leave Banbury on Friday to reach Smithfield Market on a Monday morning'. (Thomas Ward Boss).

Stock markets were held in the centre of Banbury until the 1920s-30s—cattle were sold in Bridge Street and Broad Street; pigs and fowls in compounds by the Angel Inn. Horses were tethered in Horse Fair by the Whately, and sheep and pigs opposite. The streets became muddy and dirty. In 1925 Midland Marts Limited organised cattle auctions in Grimsbury—the central position of Banbury, with its good communications by rail and road increased the importance of the auctions. Stock came from all over Southern England and even Leeds. By the 1960s Banbury had become the largest stockmarket in England and of European importance.

Until the 19th century most farmers discussed sales of corn in the Red Lion Inn (now replaced by Woolworths). Two magnificent Corn Exchanges were opened in 1857, in an unfinished state described by the Press as 'utterly unfit for business'. One was built in Cornhill by the Banbury Corn Exchange Company Limited and the other by their rivals The Central Corn Exchange Company in the market place. The Cornhill Exchange became the Vine Inn, and its facade will form the entrance to the new shopping centre, and the other became a skating rink, Blinkhorn's Picture House, and later a shopping arcade. Neither exchange was a financial success for many still found the Red Lion and the Crown more congenial.

Carriers played an important part in the trade of the town well into the 20th century. In 1838 there were 208 carriers who visited Banbury 465 times a week from 154 neighbouring towns and villages. Their work was diminished by the development of the railway network and the postal service. Villagers could hitch rides to town aboard the carts, or could get the carriers to execute commissions. Carriers would bring goods for sale from the villages and take back goods required by villagers, thus forming an important link between town and country. They were re-inforced by long distance coach traffic:

'The London waggon from Banbury was drawn by eight strong horses. It had broad wheels. A large punt or square shaped boat was suspended by chains to the bottom of the waggon between the wheels. In this punt lambs, sheep, pigs, and poultry of various sorts, were carried, being fed at intervals on the journey. In the bed of the waggon goods of a heavy character were packed three or four feet in height; on the top of these were five or six tiers consisting of butter in flats, and carcases of sheep and pigs. The size of the waggon was 18 feet in length, 7½ feet in breadth at the bottom of the waggon and 12 feet to the top of the tilt. . . . Good heavy mohair curtains securely closed up the back. Bags containing a large quantity of food for the horses hung in waterproof sheets in front. . . . Two huge horn lanterns were carried, one in front and one behind the team. Two waggoners, with massive whips, always travelled with the team'. (Thomas Ward Boss).

Banbury has always been the commercial centre for the region within a ten mile radius, colloquially known as 'Banburyshire'. The creation of a railway network in the 1850s strengthened its central position, a fact taken advantage of by the plush-weaver Joseph Ashby Gillett who ran the New Bank. He opened new branches in Witney, Oxford, Chipping Norton, Abingdon, Deddington and Bampton, in addition to the headquarters in Banbury and existing branches in Woodstock, Lower Heyford and Steeple Aston.

Shops increased in number and in the variety of their wares. Many were connected with crafts such as the tailor's shop, run by T. E. Baker. Families like the Bakers in Parson's Street lived, worked, and sold their goods on the same premises. The shopping streets were far more popular in the 19th century when shopkeepers, their families and assistants lived over the shop. Many were family businesses—multiple chain stores were unknown. A few concerns survive today, which can be traced back over generations, such as Chapmans the furnishers.

Cow fair, about a century ago.

69

ABOVE LEFT: Banbury horse fair *c*.1900.

BELOW: The sheepmarket in Horsefair, before
moving to the stockyards.

ABOVE RIGHT: Banbury Christmas Fatstock Show
1921 in Bridge Street.

70

ABOVE: Banbury Stockmarket—now the largest in Europe.

BELOW: Banbury Michaelmas Fair, early this century.

Banbury in 1838.

Corn Exchange Poster (Cheneys).

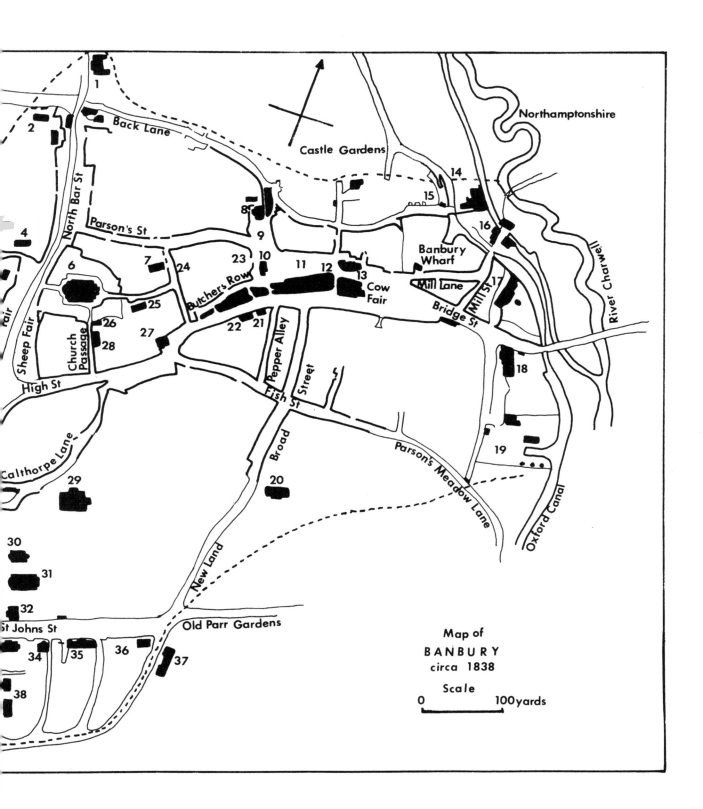

Northamptonshire

Castle Gardens

Back Lane

North Bar St

Parson's St

Sheep Fair

Church Passage

High St

Calthorpe Lane

New Land

Old Parr Gardens

St Johns St

Butcher's Row

Cow Fair

Pepper Alley

Fish St

Broad Street

Banbury Wharf

Mill Lane

Mill St

Bridge St

Parson's Meadow Lane

Oxford Canal

River Charwell

Map of
BANBURY
circa 1838

Scale

0   100 yards

ABOVE: Cornhill Corn Exchange, later 'The Vine Inn',
now an entrance to the new shopping centre.

BELOW: Banbury market in the '20's.

74

ABOVE: Banbury market *c.*1910 (Blinkhorns).

BELOW LEFT: Young bargain hunters.

BELOW RIGHT: The market today.

LEFT: Period shop façades
ABOVE RIGHT: Lamprey and Sons, 19th C merchants and
BELOW RIGHT: Hoods' early 19th C shop, both in Bridge Street.

ABOVE: Shops in the High Street, late 19th century.

BELOW LEFT: Mawles' 1890 facade in the High Street.

BELOW RIGHT: Behind the town hall—19th C mini-shop.

T. ASHWELL,

SILK MERCER, GENERAL DRAPER

FURRIER, HOSIER, & GLOVER,

63, High Street, BANBURY.

DRESSES IN GREAT VARIETY, PATTERNS FREE

Mantles, Millinery, Underclothing, Dressmaking.

| Agent for | Close at |
| Liberty's Art Fabrics. | 5 p.m. on Saturdays. |

STEAM SAW MILLS AND JOINERY WORKS
1, Warwick Road, Banbury.

W. J. BLOXHAM,
SUCCESSOR TO
CLARIDGE & BLOXHAM, late CHARLES CLARIDGE,

Builder, Contractor, & Merchant

Enquiries for all kinds of Building Materials solicited.   Prices by return post.
Estimates FREE.

Funerals personally conducted in town and country.

BAKER'S
CLOTHING ESTABLISHMENT.

Tailoring in all Branches.

READY-MADE CLOTHING of every Description.

HATS,   GLOVES,   COLLARS,
CAPS,   SHIRTS,   TIES,
HOSIERY,   BRACES,   LEGGINGS.

Anderson's Celebrated Waterproofs.

60, PARSON'S STREET, BANBURY.

G. GASCOIGNE,
Cabinet Maker, Upholsterer,
Undertaker, &c.,

MARLBOROUGH ROAD and 8, SOUTHAM ROAD, BANBURY.

Window Blinds made to order.   Venetian Blinds Re-corded and Taped.
Carpets made to order, taken up, beaten, and re-laid.

DEALER IN ANTIQUE FURNITURE
Ladies' Needlework made up to newest designs.

ALL KINDS OF REPAIRS ATTENDED TO.

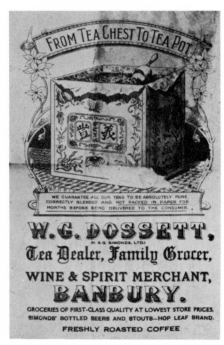

ABOVE: Cheney's Railway Guide Advertisements.

BELOW LEFT: Ernest Butler's Advertisement illustrates
Banbury's former coat of arms.
BELOW RIGHT: Dossetts used to have a shop on the corner of Parson's
Street, now replaced by a new development, but commemorated by a
plaque on the wall.

HIGH STREET, BANBURY 1856

(taken from Banbury Almanack and Local Directory for 1856)

1.	William Dickason	Tailor, Draper and Hatter.
2.	Henry Cowper	Linen and Woollen Draper and Hatter.
3.	Henry Gulliver	TALBOT INN, Hop Merchant, Retail licence, Wine Merchant, Wholesale Spirit Merchant.
4.	Nind & Co.	Grocer and Tea Dealer, Foreign Fruiterer.
5.	T. Beeseley, F.C.S.	Analytical Chemist and Druggist.
6.	Robert Kirby	Linen and Woollen Draper, Hatter.
7.	Charles Fowler	RED LION, Posting and Commercial Inn, lets Horses, Gigs, etc. for hire. Omnibus meets every L.N.W.R. railway train.
	Mrs. Fowler	Carrier, Parcels Agent to L.N.W.R.
	William Cother	Auctioneer.
8.	Robert Potter	Linen and Woollen Draper, Hatter.
9.	E. & H. Austen	Grocer and Tea Dealer, Foreign Fruiterer.
10.	David Falkner	Ready-made Clothes Shop, Tailor, Draper, Hatter.
11.	R. T. Haynes	Auctioneer.
12.	T. R. Cobb & Son	BUCKS & OXON UNION BANK.
	Miss Conworth	School teacher.
13.	E. Railton	Boot and Shoe-maker, leather cutter; lets private lodgings.
14.	Miss Smith	Grocer, Tea Dealer, Foreign Fruiterer.
15.	John Page	Perfumer and Hairdresser, Toy Dealer
16.	Mrs. Slatter	Butcher.
	Joseph Slatter	Ironmonger.
	W. Allen	Accountant.
17.	Messrs. Mosley	Surgeon Dentists.
	James Grimbly	Grocer and Tea Dealer, Foreign Fruiterer, British Wine Dealer, Scottish Equitable Life Assurance Agent, Alderman.
18.	W. P. Gilkes	Chemist and Druggist; lets private lodgings.
19.	William Holland	Gunsmith.
20.	Henry Flowers	Butcher.
21.		
22.	Misses Kimberley and Chester	Straw Bonnet Makers; establishment for milliners and dressmakers.
23.	William Hobley	Painter, Paper Hanger, Plumber and Glazier, Unity Life and Fire Assurance Agent.
24.	R. S. Wise	Surgeon.
25.	Draper & Munton	Attorneys.
	W. Munton	Phoenix Fire Assurance Agent; Pelican Life Assurance Agent.
26.	Charles Taylor	Cooper.
27.	T. J. Willis	Cabinet-maker and Upholsterer, painter and Paper-hanger, Plumber and Glazier.
28.	George Cottam	Mutual Life Assurance Agent, Painter and Paper Hanger, Plumber and Glazier, Sign-Painter and Gilder. Lets private lodgings.
29.	Mrs. Brewerton	Milliner and Dressmaker.
30.	Richard Fisher	Painter and Paper Hanger, Plumber and Glazier.
	Miss Fisher	Dressmaker and Milliner.
31.	Mrs. Potter	Butcher.
32.	James Hall	Auctioneer, Cabinet-maker and Upholsterer.
33.	Alban Armitt	Butcher.
34.	B. Evans	Ready-made Clothes Shop.
35.	Misses Page	Establishment for Milliners and Dressmakers; lets private lodgings.
	W. Rusher	Depository, Christian Knowledge Depot; Western Life Assurance Agent, Stamp Office.
36.		
37.		
38.		
39.	John Gazey	Wine Vaults, Wholesale Spirit Merchant, Retail licence, Wine Merchant.
40.	Richard Claridge	Brickmaker, Builder and Bricklayer, Carpenter.
41.	Charles Pearson	Perfumer and Hairdresser.
42.	John Kilby	Attorney; Star Life Assurance Agent.
43.	Dickens	Letter of horses, etc.
44.	R. H. Brookes	Chemist and Druggist, surgeon dentist; United Kingdom Temperance Provident Institution.
45.	John Fortescue	Clerk to Trustees of Charities; Clerk to County Court Clerk to Magistrate, Attorney; Economic Life Assurance Agent.
46.	C. H. Davids	Surveyor of Land, etc., Estate Agent.
47.	William Waters Heming	Attorney, Standard Life Assurance Agent.
48.		
49.	Wm. Brain	POST OFFICE
	Whittem, Cooper & Co.	Leather-cutters.
50.	W. Rusher	Actuary, Bank for Savings, and Government Annuity Society.
51.	Benjamin Wm. Aplin	Attorney, Clerical Life Assurance Agent.
52.	Samuel Carter	Basket and Sieve Maker, China, Glass, etc. Dealer; lets private lodgings.
	Miss Carter	Child's Teacher.
53.	David Gould	Sign Painter and Gilder and Carver.
54.	J. H. Railton	Wholesale Spirit Merchant and Wine Merchant, Grocer and Tea Dealer, British Wine Dealer, Foreign Fruiterer.
55.	Wm. Hayward	WHITE HORSE HOTEL and Commercial, Brewer, Maltster, letter of horses and gigs, etc.
56.	J. Lumbert	Tailor and Draper, and Hatter, lets private lodgings.
57.	Henry Stone	Bookseller and Stationer.
58.	Mrs. C. Rowell	Resident Householder.
	Miss Shirley	Resident Householder.
59.	Mrs. Stutterd	Woollen Draper.
60.	Samuel Humphris	Miller and Mealman.
61.	Tanner Brothers	Linen and Woollen Drapers.
62.	Moore & Judge	Attorneys, Farmers' Assurance Agents.
	Barford & Son	Coal Merchant and Corn Dealer.
63.	R. Havers	LONDON & COUNTY JOINT STOCK BANK. Minerva Life Assurance Agent, Accidental Death Assurance Agent.
64.	J. Drinkwater	WHITE LION HOTEL Posting and Commercial, Great Western Railway Company Agent, Carrier, Agent for Goding's Stout, Letter of horses, gigs, etc. Corporation Councillor Omnibus meets all G.W. Trains.
65.	J. Gardner	Ironmonger, Brazier, Tinplate worker, Gas-fitter and Bell-hander, Seed and Hop Merchant.
66.	Archibald Dods	Cabinet Maker and Upholsterer.
67.	T. H. Wyatt	STAR.
68.	Walford & Son	Watch, Clockmaker and Jeweller.
69.	J. Gilby	Miller and Mealman, Coal Merchant.
	Walford & Son	As above.
70.	W. Betts	Baker and Cake Shop.
71.	Mrs. Willitts	Perfumer and Hairdresser, Toy Dealer.
72.	George Walford	ADVERTISER OFFICE, Bookseller and Stationer, Printers; Private lodgings.
73.	T. Perry	Brickmaker, Nursery Garden and Seedsman.
74.	Miss Clarke	Establishment for Milliners and Dressmakers.
75.	Danby & Caless	Auctioneers, Surveyors of Land.
	Moore & Judge	Farmers Fire, Life and Hailstorm Assurance Office.
76.	William Strange	Linen and Woollen Draper and Hatter.
77.	John Hart	Boot and Shoe-maker.
78.	John Reiley	Confectioner, English and Foreign Fruiterer.
79.		
80.	Richard Page	Perfumer and Hairdresser.
81.		
82.		
83.		
84.	W. Payne	Watch and Clockmaker, Jeweller, Stationer.
85.	Thomas Rathbone	Butcher.
86.	Charles Collins	Hatter.
87.	George White	Boot and Shoe-maker.
88.	Robert Stevens	Grocer and Tea Dealer, Foreign Fruiterer, British Wine Dealer.
89.	G. Webb	Boot and Shoe-maker.
90.	&	Watch and Clock Maker, Jeweller, Umbrellas,
91.	J. H. Durran	Dealer in fancy pipes and cigars.
	Mrs. Durran	Straw Bonnet Maker.
	Misses Durran	Milliners and Dressmakers.
92.	John Tooley	Eating House and Sausage Maker.
93.	Mrs. Powell	Pork Butcher, Eating House and Sausage Maker.
94.	John Claridge	Wholesale Spirit Merchant, Retail Licence Wine Merchant.
95.	John Morrey	SHIP.

Also lived in High Street.

Mrs. Viggers	Eating House and Sausage Maker, Register Office for Servants.
W. P. Payne	Dissenters and General Assurance Agent.
George Gardner	London Assurance Agent.
John Conworth	Resident Householder.
Lees & Co.	Plush Manufacturers.
G. B. Cricket	Ready-made Clothes Shop, Linen and Woollen Draper, Hatter.
F. J. Archer	Teacher attending families—music and singing.

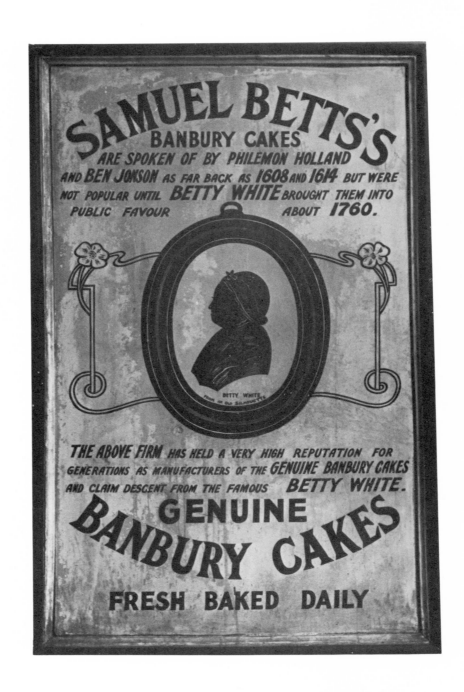

The Betts Cake Shop sign (Banbury Museum).

Cakes, Cheese and Ale

'Stile it I might Banberrie of the North
. . . Famous for twanging ale, zeale, cakes and cheese.'
(Richard Braithwait in 'A Strappado for the Divell', 1615).

Banbury cheese and ale were mentioned in mediaeval times, but the cakes, now the most famous commodity, were first referred to by Thomas Bright in his 'Treatise of Melancholie', published in 1586: 'Sodden wheat is a grosse and melancholicke nourishment and bread especially of the fine flower [flour] unleavened. Of this sort are bag puddings made with flower, fritters, pancakes, such as we call Banberrie Cakes, and the great ones are confected with butter, eggs, etc; used at weddings, and however it be prepared rye and bread made thereof carried with it plenty of melancholie.'

In 1615 Gervase Markham referred to Banbury cakes in his 'English Huswife'. By this time the cakes were probably similar to today, with currants. They are mentioned by Lord Carleton, writing to Secretary Conway in 1627, concerning troop movements. 'if it succeeds not so well where they are going, the Berkshire soldiers will be well content to eat Banbury Cake.' In 1638 the Earl of Manchester wrote; 'My son's nurse is of a spiced conscience, made of a Banbury cake.'

Ben Jonson in 'Bartholomew Fair' (1614) wrote about a Banbury baker:

Littlewit: 'Rabbi Busy, sir; he is more than an elder, he is a prophet, sir.'
Quarlous: 'O, I know him! a baker, is he not?'
Littlewit: 'He *was* a baker, sir, but he does dream now, and see visions; he has given over his trade.'
Quarlous: 'I remember that too; out of a scruple he took, that, in spiced conscience, those Cakes he made were served to bridales, maypoles, morrisses, and such profane feasts and meetings. His christen name is Zeal-of-the-Land.'

This may well have referred to an actual person, Richard Busby who owned the Original Cake Shop at that time, and was presumably a strong Puritan.

The first cake maker we know by name is Edward Welchman, who made cakes at 'The Signe of the Unicorne' in Parson's Street in 1638 but the fame of Banbury cakes is really due to Betty White and her husband Jarvis, who baked in Banbury in the mid 18th century. Betty was jealous of her reputation and used to say 'My name is quiet Betty, I never meddles nor makes with anybody, no mealman never calls on me twice'. She too suffered from rising prices: 'Only think, there's currans, they be twice the price th' used to be, and then there's butter an' sugar they be double the price th' was formerly'. Her husband Jarvis, who reputedly spent most of his time leaning over the shop door, proudly maintained that his wife's cakes were so light that a sparrow could fly off with one in its beak. Betty and Jarvis owned the Original Cake Shop, which was subsequently taken over by John and Daniel Rutter, Samuel Beesley, and Mrs E. W. Brown in 1872. William Betts made cakes in the High Street in the early 19th century, and Daniel Claridge had a shop in Parson's Street. William Betts was a grandson of Betty White. His sons Samuel and Alfred took over his business, and Alfred later opened a shop at 85 High Street.

The cake trade flourished in the 19th century—in 1838 a consignment was sent to India, in 1840 Samuel Beesley sold 139,500 two-penny cakes and even more in 1841. He sent orders to America and Australia. When the railway reached Banbury, cakes were regularly sold on the station platform. Queen Victoria was presented with a box of Banbury cakes when she visited the town.

Special cake boxes were made for the firms who made Banbury cakes, some in the shape of the cakes, some replicas of the Original Cake Shop and others with the silhouettes of Betty and Jarvis White and drawings illustrating legends connected with the cakes. The Loveridge family of Neithrop specialised in making chip willow baskets for packing them and these were often used at fairs. Sadly, the Original Cake Shop was demolished in 1968.

We first learn of Banbury cheese in 1430, when fourteen such cheeses were among the provisions sent to France for the Duke of Bedford's household. Also in the 15th century William Bulleyn, in his 'Book of Compoundes' mentions Banbury cheese as being of special excellence. Thomas Cromwell was given two types—hard and soft, in 1533 and 1538. Banbury Corporation Accounts of 1556 mention eight shillings paid 'for vj copull of Ches y^t wer seunt to London'. Burton praises the cheese in 'Anatomy of Melancholy' (1586) 'of all cheeses, I take that kind which we call Banbury Cheese to be the best'. Shakespeare refers to it in the 'Merry Wives of Windsor' when Bardolph calls Slender a 'Banbury Cheese' because of his thinness. In 1601, in 'Jack Dunn's Entertainment': 'Put off your clothes and you are like a Banbury cheese, Nothing but paring'. There are several other later references to it by Dr Plot, Sir Joseph Williamson and Horace Walpole, and in Defoe's Tour it is said that Banbury 'has a considerable trade, especially in Cheese, as all the country round is a rich feeding meadow ground'.

A 16th century manuscript in the Bodleian Library describes the cheese:
'Take a thin ches fat, and hote mylk, as it comes from the Cow. And Pyre it forth withal in Somertyme. And kned your Couddes bot ones and kned them not to smal bot breke them ones with your hondes And in Somertyme salt the Couddes nothying but let the Chese lye iij dayes unsalted And then salt them, And lay oon upon an other but not to much salt. And so shall they gether butter. And in Wynter tyme in lyke wyse bot then hote your mylk. And salt your Couddes for then it will gether butter of itself. Take the Wrunge Whey of ye same mylk and let it stand a day or ij til it have a Creme, and it shall make as good butter as anyother.'

Beesley describes it in the 19th century: 'A very rich kind of Cheese is yet made in the neighbourhood of Banbury, at a late season of the year, on some very rich pasture land; and this may possibly be the kind for which the town was formerly so highly celebrated. It is almost white, about one inch in thickness, and resembles in appearance the soft cream cheese which is made in many parts; but it is of far more delicious taste, and bears the high price of 1s 6d per pound when new, or about 1s 9d when ripe. It is generally called in the neighbourhood "latter-made cheese", as it can only be made after Michaelmas. A considerable quantity of this cheese is yet sent to different parts, each cheese packed in its separate basket.'

Thomas Ward Boss describes a Cheese Fair in Banbury:

'Banbury was highly celebrated for its Cheese Fair. Very early on the morning after Michaelmas Fair, a large number of farmers' waggons and other vehicles began to arrive from Warwickshire, Worcestershire and other districts, and large cargoes of cheese might have been seen stacked all over the Cornhill. Great commercial activity prevailed in this part of the Fair during the day. Our local cheesemakers and many others from a large district were busily engaged tasting, weighing, buying and carting away to the purchasers' warehouses and consigning to other towns. This fair in Banbury has ceased to exist since the middle of the 19th century.'

The cheese made at the end of the 19th century at Spital Farm was described as a 'Shrivelled wrinkled looking thing, looked like a cheese made out of season'. Trade in Banbury cheese declined rapidly—although Richard Pococke wrote of Banbury's 'great trade in cheese' in 1786; by 1851 people could scarcely remember it.

Banbury Ale has evidently been renowned since the middle ages—in 1265, Eleanor, Countess of Leicester employed a Banbury ale wife in Odiham, Hampshire, and the 'Lex Anglicana Perantique' of 1320-30, which contains a list of 108 English towns mentioning local products, refers to brewing in Banbury. Seventeenth century rhymes refer to Banbury ale but there are no other references to it being sold outside the town in the 16th and 17th centuries. By the 19th century brewing was increasingly important—in 1823 three maltsters are recorded; by 1852 there were 14. George Herbert refers to small scale brewing:

'And this brings me to the brewers who were bakers as well; the two trades were considered as one. The bakers generally had large back premises, and most of them had a brewery attached, so that a person would send his malt to the brewer and tell him how many gallons he required to the bushel of malt. It was then brewed and carried home and turned into his own barrels, but most persons used to have their own plant at home: the baker was then employed at home to brew for them.'

The most important brewery in the first half of the 19th century was that of Richard Austin, who had taken over the business from his father-in-law, James Barnes, the canal engineer. Their brewery was in North Bar. In 1814 he had a hop garden, two malthouses, ten inns in Banbury and thirteen in the surrounding area, with a total value of £37,000. Their beer was sent as far as Birmingham, Brierly Hill, London and India. Richard Austin played a prominent role in Banbury life—he had a large house built in The Green and he provided a chapel for the Calvinist baptists.

In 1807 the brewery which later became Hunt Edmunds was founded when a Cropredy farmer, Thomas Hunt, moved into premises in the 'Unicorn'. In 1847 he moved to Bridge Street where there was already a malthouse. Three years later Edmunds became a partner and between then and 1866 the brewery was enlarged.

One hundred and fourteen tied houses in the Banbury area were bought together with the Banbury Brewery Company in Bridge Street, and in 1884 'The Sun' brewery in Old Parr Road. They took on 50 more tied houses, and later bought Hudson's Witney Brewery and Hunts of Burford. In 1918 they purchased the only surviving brewery in Banbury—Messrs Drinnell and Co, which had once been Austins Brewery but in 1967 brewing in Banbury ceased when the brewery was taken over by Mitchell and Butler and it has since been demolished.

The other main brewery in Banbury was that of T. H. Wyatt, built in the 1830s in Bridge Street.

The drinksellers and public houses played an important role in Banbury life. The public houses formed the hub of the local transport system. In 1837 five important coaching routes converged on the White Lion and another on the Red Lion.

Drinksellers were also prominent in local politics—the Red and White Lion were usually Tory, and Samuel Glaze of the Butcher's Arms and the Old George was a staunch Liberal.

Institutions such as the Banbury Association for the Prosecution of Felons held meetings in inns. The Three Tuns, now the Whately Hotel, had a multiple role in the late 18th century as Excise Office, Post Office, and venue for assemblies, balls, parties and concerts. Pub business was particularly good on fair days and club days and travelling entertainers performed. Not surprisingly, drunkenness and violence became widespread, which encouraged the temperance movement, largely associated with the middle classes, and linked with aristocratic control over Banbury. This movement flourished in the town in the mid 19th century.

After the arrival of the railway in Banbury, which rapidly destroyed the coaching trade, inns became less important, but the Red and White Lion took advantage of the situation, becoming agents for the London North Western Railway and the Great Western Railway respectively. Water supplies improved, and the temperance movement faded, but inns still remained an important part of Banbury life.

The Reindeer is the oldest inn in Banbury; we first find it called 'The Reindeer' in 1664, but the building dates back to the mid 16th century when it was a stone building with a timber framed front to the upper storey. The front block and a three-storey wing were added in 1570, together with the magnificent gates with their inscription 'IOHN-KNIGHT + IHONE-KNIGHT + DAVID-HORN. ANNO DIN 1570'. John Knight himself was a man of property and his family was prominent in Banbury throughout the 17th century. A datestone of 1624 indicates that an extra room was added then, and the Globe Room was added in 1637, marking the peak of the inn's prosperity. Its architecture is of high quality with ovolo sectioned mullioned windows, which are only known in important buildings in the area at that date, and fine ornamental panelling made especially for the room. The origin of the name Globe Room is uncertain but it may have contained a globe of the world. The inn declined, as it was in an unsuitable position for coaching, and by 1871 was considered fit by William Mewburn of Wickham Park only as a place to entertain the workmen who had been rebuilding his house. In the early 20th century the panelling was removed, and was thought to have been exported to America. It was rediscovered by the Banbury Historical Society, bought back by the Banbury Borough Council, and is now in the museum.

The other major 17th century inn still standing is the Unicorn, situated in the Market Place—first recorded as an inn in 1676, although built around 1648.

THE BETTS FAMILY RECIPE FOR BANBURY CAKES

Ingredients

Pastry:	8 lbs flour	4 pints milk
	8 lbs butter	1 oz yeast
Filling:	40 lbs currants	1 pint rose water
	5 lbs peel	1 oz nutmeg
	10 lbs sugar	4 lbs butter
	¼ pint brandy	6 lbs flour
	½ pint rum	

Mix a light flaky pastry and let it stand for six hours.
Mix the ingredients for the filling in the same way as you would make mincemeat. Make it into rolls.
Roll out the pastry and put the filling inside. Mould into shape and glaze with castor sugar and milk.
Bake the cakes in a fairly quick oven until they are brown, watching them carefully while they are baking.
Cakes were usually made in batches of 100 dozen. The traditional shape has the crust rising into a dome.

ABOVE LEFT: Jarvis White (Mrs Hughes).

CENTRE LEFT: The shop in the High Street used by both the Betts and the Browns.

BELOW LEFT: Betts Banbury Cake box.

ABOVE RIGHT: The original cake shop in Parson's Street, demolished in 1969.

CENTRE RIGHT: A Banbury cake basket.

BELOW RIGHT: The men's bake house at the original cake shop.

ABOVE: Brown's cake box in the shape of the Parson's Street shop.
CENTRE: Tiles in Wincolls Bakery at Bridge Street,
 advertising Banbury Cakes.
BELOW: Both sides of the Reindeer token.

ABOVE: A Banbury cake float at Queen Victoria's Jubilee (Blinkhorns).

BELOW: Hunt Edmunds Brewery (painting by Maurice Draper).

87

Wh

ABOVE RIGHT: The

ABOVE LEFT: The
(painting

BELOW

CENTRE BELOW: Local jars a

BELOW RIGHT: Wrought

88

ken.

its restoration in 1974.

Wheel, now demolished
e Draper).

ite Lion.

ater bottles (Banbury Museum).

of The Albion, by the canal.

ABOVE: Red Lion and BELOW: its courtyard—
once the scene of Thursday corn markets.

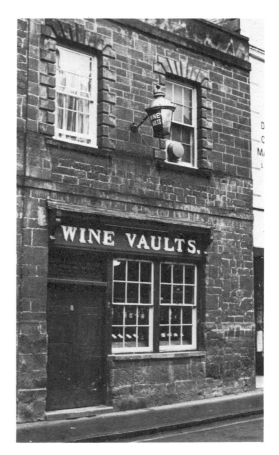

ABOVE LEFT: Castle Vaults, a fine example of polychrome brickwork by William Wilkinson, built in 1866.

ABOVE RIGHT: The Wine Vaults, Parson's Street.

BELOW LEFT: The Reindeer.

BELOW RIGHT: The Globe Room as it once was—in the Reindeer Inn.

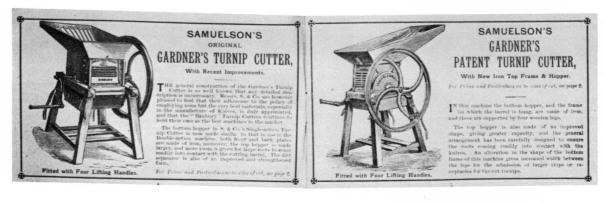

ABOVE: Model of a plush loom (Banbury Museum).

CENTRE: William Rusher's token.

BELOW: From Samuelson's publicity leaflet (Cheneys).

From Plush to Turnip Cutters

Good things to engross
Near Banbury Cross
Where Tommy shall go on the nag.
He makes no mistake,
Buys a Banbury Cake,
Books, Pictures and Banbury Shag.

Banbury has been closely connected with textiles since the middle ages, and by the 17th century textile industries were well established. In the 15th century there was a wool market and by the 16th century a wole-house is mentioned and the town was famous for its 'blue bonnets'—woollen berets. By the 17th century there were clothiers, dyers, fullers and weavers in Banbury and the surrounding area, making broadcloth, worsted and linen. Wool was brought to the wool warehouse in North Bar to be baled.

Road improvements of the 18th century increased horse drawn traffic which stimulated Banbury's webbing and horse cloth industry. In 1701 Messrs Cobb set up a webbing and horse cloth factory in Banbury, employing mostly yeomen, who owned their own land, fulling mills, looms or dye-vats. Cobb's products were sent to Birmingham, Walsall and Bristol. The number of persons employed in 1838 was about 40. The weavers were chiefly men and boys, but there were five girls weaving light articles. The average weekly earnings of the boys winding were then 1s 0½d and of the weavers by piecework were 11s 0¾d; they worked on an average 9½ hours per day for six days in the week.

The last girth factory in Banbury, that of Mr Mead, closed in 1932. A wide variety of textiles was made on a small scale in the town, including hemp dressing, silk and linen weaving, jersey weaving and lacemaking.

However, from 1750 by far the most important manufacturer was that of Banbury shag, or plush, a fabric similar to velvet. It was complex, requiring over 30 processes for certain types.

Plush was usually dyed after weaving and was washed in ponds and hung on racks to dry in Water Lane. A weaver could make 42-44 yards of livery plush a month, and would receive about £3 for his pains.

Several different types of plushes were made—livery, silk and worsted. Livery plush was hand woven and expensive. Queen Victoria's servants wore royal blue livery plush, her foresters in Windsor Forest and Richmond Park wore Windsor green waistcoats, and the royal footmen had scarlet knee breeches. Russia ordered blue, black and white; Italy, Madonna blue; Spain, yellow and blue. Other countries supplied included USA, China and Turkey. Locally, the huntsmen's coats of the Heythrop Hunt were dark blue.

Silk plush was produced in over 300 shades, mostly for export. The Persian court wore petunia and green, and the Japanese ordered silk plush for their winter kimonos. Plush printed in garish colours, sometimes embroidered with sequins, and waterproofed against tropical storms, was sent to Africa to be made into dresses for the natives; much was made in three yard lengths, folded in half, a hole cut in the top for the head, and seams sewn down the sides. Silk plush was also used for upholstery.

Worsted plush was made largely for industrial use, in several different qualities. Some was used for raising the nap of the cloth for friction gloves used by athletes and in Turkish baths. A special plush with a narrow red stripe was used in the manufacture of Irish linen. Much worsted plush was dyed a green colour, easy on the eyes. Other worsted plushes were used in place of rabbit fur in printing, in seed sorting, tobacco packing, and life-saving apparatus. Black plush was used for straining gold, and light pastel shades for powder puffs. Mohair plush was made to exclude light from photographic lenses. It was also used for draught excluders. A heavy pile plush developed for making coats, was adapted to make rugs, which were hard wearing. Carpets were sewn together by hand for big houses—these were made only for special orders. Curtains and cushions were also made by hand.

In 1831 about 550 people were employed in the industry, including women and children. The main firms were Gillett, Lees & Gillett (150 looms), T. & T. Baughan (120 looms) and Harris (160 looms). The only other centres in England making plush for clothing were Manchester, Coventry and Kettering. In the years of prosperity the weavers were the aristocrats of the working class, educated and fairly well off, but by 1851 they had been reduced to the status of agricultural labourers as the plush industry declined, as competition from Coventry increased.

The decline of Gilletts was partially staved off by their purchase of the Bessemer embossing machine, which used heat to fuse a pattern on to the fabric. It was used for upholstery for rooms in Windsor Castle, but eventually was reduced to providing upholstery for omnibuses and cabs, although special designs were made for the House of Commons and the House of Lords. To combat the stiff competition Thomas Baughan opened a factory for worsted and mohair spinning. Cubitts, who took over from Gilletts, continued to make Banbury plush until 1909. They sold their business to Wrenches of Shutford where it continued until 1948.

The other major industry in Banbury in the 19th century was that of agricultural engineering, which still linked Banbury with its surrounding area, although capturing a far wider market. James Gardner, who laid the foundation of the industry, had an ironmongers' shop in the High Street and was an engineer and inventor patenting machines for cutting hay and straw in 1815, and a fat cutter for use in candle making in 1841. His tour-de-force was his turnip cutter, invented in 1834, which was said never to be bettered and continued to be manufactured until the Britannia works closed down in 1933. Two years after Gardner's death in 1846 the business was purchased by Bernhard Samuelson, an engineer whose railway works in Tours had been closed due to the French Revolution of 1848. He founded the Britannia Works in Fish Street.

It was Bernhard Samuelson who changed Banbury from a market town to an industrial centre. His business grew from small beginnings—his wage bill for the first week was £32, he had 27 workmen and acted as his own manager, traveller and correspondent. Gradually his business expanded and he patented more implements. By 1860, according to the Great Western Railway Guide:

'Banbury is as famous for its production of agricultural implements as for its cross and its cakes . . .'.

The Britannia Works occupied three sites—'Upper' (the site of the original shop), 'Canal Side' and 'Lower' connected by a tramway. The sites contained a drilling shop, erecting shop, mower fitting shop, etc. Areas of new housing for the workers grew up in the Cherwell area and Grimsbury. The machines produced included McCormick reapers (under licence from America), digging and forking machines, patent reaping machines, and lawn mowers as well as turnip cutters. The firm even built the railway viaduct at Hook Norton. The Patent Digging or Forking Machine won a silver medal from the Royal Agricultural Society in 1853 and received the following testimonial from a farmer, Edward Woollet Wilmot:

'I have tried your "Digger" and find it answer thoroughly. I put it to work in some strong and very foul land which had been ploughed once and was very hard and dry, it pulverised it well and brought everything to the surface. I have no doubt the "Digger" will prove a very efficient and economical implement.'

In the depression of the late 1870s Samuelson was forced to lay off men. Banbury was severely affected by the bad harvests and general depression in agriculture, partially caused by imports of cheap grain into the country. Despite the depression, the firm of Samuelsons continued in production until 1933 and for a time in the 19th century almost cornered the world market.

The town had several other engineering works, including Lampitt's Vulcan Foundry and Barrow's Cherwell Works which survived into the 20th century.

Printing in Banbury dates from the 18th century. John Cheney, who ran the Unicorn Inn, took up publishing around 1766. By 1767 he was selling ale and French brandy while supplying ballads by the ream. His success so aroused the jealousy of Oxford printers that he was prosecuted for doing business without serving an apprenticeship. He overcame this problem by apprenticing himself to his journeyman, John Madegan, while continuing the business. By 1788 it was flourishing so he left the Unicorn for larger premises, advertising himself as a copper-plate printer, bookseller and stationer, selling Bibles, bodkins, godly books and garters, 'playing cards as cheap as in London', newspapers and lottery tickets. He and his sons, John and Thomas, printed Articles of Friendly Societies, sermons, chapbooks, broadsides and ballads. The firm is still in business.

Another printer, John Golby Rusher, adapted many rhymes and stories to Banbury, and became known for his children's literature.

Other printers in the 19th century included Henry Stone, who manufactured a patent box file, and Potts, who in 1838 produced the Banbury Guardian, Banbury's first newspaper.

There were, too, many small crafts and industries such as basket making, straw plaiting, straw-hat making. Bee skeps were made locally. George Herbert:

'Fiddler Claridge . . . and his son . . . used to make bee-hives. . . . In the summer they would take a large knife and cut briars. They were of a certain kind; not the round briars which bear hips, but such as bear blackberries. After being trimmed from prickles, they were split down into two or three parts. They had then a piece of thick leather placed upon their knee, and scraped down with a knife until they were almost like a piece of whalebone and as elastic. These were used for sewing the straw together.'

Other small crafts included chair making, tailoring, coopering, cork burning, clay pipe making, mop making, and the manufacture of grandfather clock cases, leather crafts (in 1851 Banbury had 29 master shoemakers and five saddlers), tanning, and with the completion of the Oxford Canal, boatbuilding. The dry dock in Herbert Tooley's boatyard in

Banbury dates from c 1790, and he carries on the boatbuilding tradition by repairing wooden narrow boats today.

A curious manufacture was that of blacking; George Herbert:

'Robert Cockerill thought that by making a cheap blacking the people might be inclined to polish their boots instead of greasing them. He therefore introduced a paste-blacking which he did up in small gallipots. . . . It then only required a little water or vinegar to make it usable. These gallipots were sold at 3d each, and after some time he started making the penny packets. . . . The blacking became celebrated through the whole of this country.'

Communications gradually improved, encouraging local industries and enabling Banbury to look beyond its immediate area. The Oxford Canal from Coventry to Oxford reached Banbury in 1789 and Oxford eleven years later. The price of coal was halved overnight, as it could now come direct from the midland coalfields, instead of having to come by sea from the north of England, then up the Thames. Heavy goods could be carried long distances far more easily by water than by road. Even before the railways reached Banbury in 1850 the coach routes led to the nearest stations, foreshadowing the revolution in transport brought about by the railways. Both the LNWR and the GWR had stations in Banbury. The town became far more important as a market and regional centre because of the railways.

ABOVE RIGHT: The erecting shop in Samuelson's Works.

ABOVE LEFT: Cobb's girth cloth mill, built in 1837. In 1870 it was taken over by the Banbury Tweed Company.

BELOW: Winding and weaving at the Banbury Plush Works.

ABOVE: The patent certificate granted to Joseph Gardner
for his turnip cutter invention.

BELOW: Samuelson's Lawn mower (Banbury Museum).

ABOVE: John Cheney's account book for 1767, while he ran his printing business in conjunction with the Unicorn.

LEFT: Turnip cutter (Oxfordshire County Museum).

BELOW RIGHT: Esther Cheney's circular letter to her customers in 1821.

J. CHENEY,

LETTER-PRESS and COPPER-PLATE

PRINTER,

BOOK-SELLER, STATIONER,

And PRINT-SELLER:

In Red-Lion Street, *Banbury, Oxon:*

Sells the following Articles on the moft reafonable terms,

WHOLESALE and RETAIL.

BIBLES, Teftaments and Common Prayer Books
Dictionaries, Spelling Books and Reading made Eafy's
Pfalms and Hymns—Dr. Watts's, Lady Huntingdon's, &c.
Ledgers and Day Books of various forts, or made to any pattern
Accompt and Copy Books
Memorandum Books for the Pocket, in Leather or Marble Paper
Battledores and Childrens Books of amufement, of various forts and prices
Pocket Books of all forts, in Red, Green and Black Morocco, common Leather and Parchment
Morocco Thread-Cafes and Balloon Purfes
Writing Paper, plain, gilt, and black edged
Meffage Cards of different kinds
Playing Cards as cheap as in LONDON
Variety of Packs of Converfation Cards
Cartridge and Shop Paper
Marble and Stained Paper
Emboffed and Box Paper
Paper hangings

Cedar Pencils and India Rubber
Beft Dutch Sealing Wax
Wafers of different forts and colours
Pens and Quills
Writing Ink
Pafteboards for Bonnets and Book-binding
Stamps for Bills and Receipts
Slip and Sheet Ballads
Godly Books and Patters
Chriftmas Carols
Hiftories and Collections
Three fheet Maps and Prints
Two fheet ditto and ditto
Prints on Royal Paper and Wood Cuts
Lotteries and Copper-plate Songs
Drawing Books and Mezzotinto Prints
Variety of elegant gilt Picture Frames
Blank Warrants, Orders of Removal, Certificates, &c. &c.
Knitting Cotton and Sewing Silk
Thread, Tape and Bindings
Pins and Needles
Thimbles and Hat Pins
Garters, Laces and Bodkins
With many Articles not here mentioned.

Almanacks, Court Kalendars, Ladies and Gentlemens Diaries, and Pocket Books, &c.

All kinds of Books, Stationary, Magazines, and other Monthly and Weekly Publications, at the advertifed Prices.

N. B. Catalogues, Club Articles, Shop and Hand-Bills, Cards, &c. &c. Printed in the neateft manner, on the fhorteft notice, and the moft reafonable terms.

Books neatly Bound, Gilt, and Lettered.

INSURANCES taken in for the PHŒNIX FIRE-OFFICE.

☞ J. CHENEY, *junior*, refpectfully informs Ladies and Gentlemen, that he takes the moft perfect Likeneffes in Miniature, Profile; painted on Glafs in a superior ftyle of elegance, which will endure for Ages: at *Five Shillings* each; in neat gilt Frames, complete. Specimens may be feen by applying to the faid J. C.—Likewife writing on Show-Boards, Signs, &c. performed by him in the neateft manner.

LEFT: John Cheney's wares.

RIGHT: Children's literature published by Rushers (Banbury Museum).

ABOVE LEFT: Rusher's Spelling Book.
BELOW: Gillett's Banbury Bank note (Banbury Museum).
ABOVE RIGHT: A Banbury ropemaker.

ABOVE: Herbert Tooley, at work in his boatyard.

BELOW LEFT: A dredger on the Oxford Canal
(photo by Martin Gelling).

BELOW RIGHT: 19th century carriers in the market place.

101

REGULATOR
Post Coach.

J. Drinkwater, jun.

RETURNS thanks to his Friends and the Public in general, for the very liberal encouragement he has met with, since he has taken to the above concern; and most respectfully informs them, that his Coach leaves the George and Dragon Inn, *Banbury*,

EVERY MORNING

at half-past Nine o'Clock; to the Craven-Arms Inn, *Southam*, at half-past Eleven; to Copps's-Hotel, and Crown Inn, *Leamington*, at 20 minutes before One; to the Castle Inn, *Warwick*, at One; and at the Castle, and Saracen's-Head Inns, *Birmingham*, early the same Evening.——Returns from *Birmingham*, every Morning at Eight o'Clock; *Warwick*, at One; *Leamington*, at 20 minutes past One; *Southam*, at half-past Two; *Banbury*, at 10 minutes before Five; and to *Oxford*, at half-past Eight in the Evening.

☞ The above Coach, meets at *Warwick*, a Coach that starts immediately to *Coventry*, *Bedworth*, *Nuneaton*, *Hinkley*, and *Earl-Shilton*, to the Three-Cranes Inn, *Leicester*, where it arrives precisely at Eight o'Clock the same Evening.

8th *MAY*, 1819.

T. CHENEY, PRINTER, BANBURY.

ABOVE LEFT: Public transport in 1819.

ABOVE RIGHT AND CENTRE: GW and L&NWR stations, Banbury; a rapid transit revolution!

BELOW LEFT: Banbury, busy line.

BELOW RIGHT: 'Modern' passengers at Banbury Station.

Government of the People

Hey diddle diddle, the Cat and the Fiddle,
The Poll Book dropped from the Moon;
But M . . . l can't laugh, for he sees no sport
In P . . . n's turning out such a spoon.

Despite having burgage tenure, its own portmoot and markets and fairs Banbury did not become a real borough until 1554 when a charter was granted by Queen Mary, with the additional privilege of electing a member of Parliament, as reward for supporting her during the Duke of Northumberland's rebellion. A pageant, a play and elaborate dinner (of capons, geese, conies, wine, pears and ale, sach & malmsey) was held to celebrate. The manorial borough disappeared and twelve aldermen and twelve chief burgesses demonstrated their new function by moving the cage and other punitive instruments from the castle to the court hall and by repaving the market place. The council had authority to hold markets and fairs, courts of pie powder and record, frankpledge, assize of bread, wine and ale, felons' and fugitives' goods and waifs and strays. They could appoint justices of the peace, make bye-laws, buy land to the value of £20 and use a common seal. The seal used in 1556 was a three branched rose or vine with flowers, on a stand with the letters BA and the motto THYS YS THE SEALE OF THE TOWNE OF BANBURY. Later, in 1584, this was replaced by the more familiar sun in splendour on an ornamental shield, still incorporated into the modern arms of the borough, with the legend SIGILLUM BURGI DE BANBURY DOMINUS NOBIS SOL ET SCUTUM. Each year the council had to elect a serjeant at mace, constables, bridgemasters, two town wardens, two auditors, two chamberlains, leather sealers, tasters, a town crier, a clerk of the beam and toll gatherers. The 1608 Charter gave Banbury a Mayor, High Steward, Recorder, Chamberlain and Town Clerk. Income from tolls, fines, rents, piccage and stallage, sale of felons' goods, bequests, wood beam and miscellaneous sources was often insufficient to cover expenditure, and in 1835 the corporation was forced to sell the maces and plate to pay its debts.

The 1832 Reform Act released the town from the patronage of the North family. Ratepayers of three years' standing elected the twelve councillors, giving the beginnings of democratic control. The council was concerned with markets and fairs, and administering justice, the gaol, and police and municipal property, and in 1889 it took on the functions of the Paving Commissioners, and the Board of Health. National Elections were treated in a far more lively way than today. Many rhymes were written about the candidates, and towards the end of the century the candidates in council elections were compared with racehorses, given nicknames and 'form'.

The gaol was in the market place—its records show some of the crimes committed and the severe punishments:

Banbury Tithe Map 1842 (Bodleian Library).

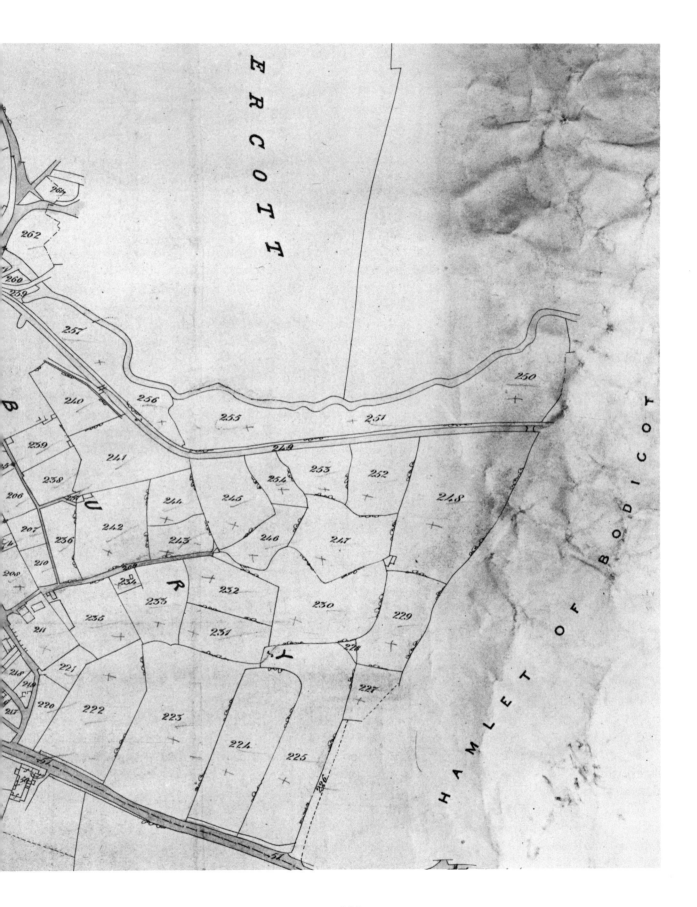

105

Jan. 27 1831	Sarah Grey bro^t by D. Claridge on Charge of taking Tea from Mr J. Drury's Shop and Cheese from Mr. Kirkby's.	

Jan. 27 1831   Sarah Grey bro^t by D. Claridge on Charge of taking Tea from Mr J. Drury's Shop and Cheese from Mr. Kirkby's.
(She was sentenced to seven years' transportation).

July 29   Ann Dixon 19 and Louisa Norman 20 bro^t round from the Cage and Com'd (committed) for one Month for disturbing the streets in the Night.

Oct. 30 1832   Powers bro^t by Thompson and Hale on Charge of stealing a Spoon and Glass at the Angel.

The Matchseller 'Old Mettle' did not always keep on the right side of the law:

April 21 1835   Willm Castle alias Mettle bro^t from the Cage by R. Butler on Charge of break^g W. Grimbley's Windows.

April 23   Mettle taken to the Office and Ordered to sit in the Stocks four hours.

The stocks, pillory and whipping post stood near Christchurch in George Street. The whipping post was a pillory 14 feet high, and the culprit had to stand on a platform with his head through the board, and his hands in shackles. The crowd pelted culprits with rotten eggs and garbage. The Cuttle Brook flowed down Parson's Street and formed a ducking pool in the market place, where scolds, fraudulent bakers and pickpockets were ducked until 1830 when a woman died in the stool.

The municipal police force was set up in 1836 consisting of six watchmen, four petty constables, two constables and a superintendent. Sarah Beesley remembers the watchmen patrolling the town, 'lantern in hand, during the night, informing the drowsy inhabitants of the hour and the state of the weather, by calling out in a gruff sing-song manner. I well recollect seeing a light from the watchman's large lantern pass along the window and hearing him say "Half-past four o'clock and a cloudy morning".'

Parish officers administered money from charities for the poor and Overseers of the poor were appointed. Poverty was a problem which cost local inhabitants nearly 25 shillings a head in 1821. The first Banbury workhouse was in Scalding Lane, later moved to South Bar, with another in Gould's Square, Neithrop. In 1803 relief was paid to 94 adults and 185 children in addition to that given to the 50 inmates of the workhouse.

The system of poor relief was so unpopular that relieving officers were mobbed and when a workhouse caught fire paupers refused to help quench the blaze. Those in the workhouse had food, clothes, medical and burial expenses provided and children were taught to read and learn their catechism. They had meat six days a week in 1795 and probably ate better than those receiving out-relief. They earned a little by spinning and twisting for local manufacturers.

The town was filthy in the 19th century. In 1825 the Paving Commissioners commenced a clean-up campaign by requesting householders to have the pavements by their property swept before 9 am three times a week, empty privies at night, clear dung from the street and provide gutters. Drainage was installed but the polluting effluent ran into the River Cherwell and millers and neighbouring property owners complained. So a sewage farm was established. The well water was hard, and soft pump water could be purchased at a half-penny a bucket in High Street and Butchers Row before the water works were established in 1854.

The Horton Infirmary was founded in 1872 provided by Mary Horton of Middleton Cheney. A Provident Dispensery enabled poorer people to pay a small weekly sum towards their treatment.

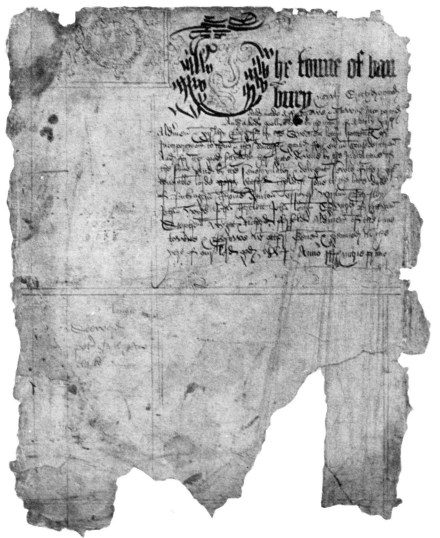

Arms of the Corporation.

ABOVE : Proclamation of Queen Mary's Charter
of 1554 (Banbury Library).

Queen Mary's Charter of 1554

(Banbury Museum).

107

ABOVE LEFT: Silver disc presented by Col. Stockton in 1932, possibly one of the objects sold by the Corporation in 1835, and engraved with the borough arms (The Charter Trustees).

ABOVE RIGHT: The 18th century town hall.

BELOW: The second town hall, built c.1590, drawn by J. Cheney in 1764. (Banbury Library).

ABOVE: Remains of the 18th century town hall, now a warehouse in Lower Cherwell Street.

RIGHT: Mallet used for beating the bounds.

BELOW: The present town hall, built in 1854 and designed by Edward Bruton of Oxford.

ABOVE: The Mayor, Councillor W. T. Palmer, beating the bounds in 1932.

LEFT: High Constable S. Stripling (Banbury Museum).

RIGHT: Reform Demonstration parade (John Cheney).

BELOW: Token issued to firemen after about three-quarters of an hour at the hand pump. It would be exchanged at a nearby inn for refreshment and redeemed by the Chief Officer after the fire had been dealt with.

Banbury Fashions for July,

FROM

"PYE'S ENTERTAINING MUSEUM,

AND

Compendium of *Useful* Knowledge."

"H. J. P. has also made a discovery likely to be of great utility in these hard times, of giving a knap and gloss to *Turned Coats*, so that they may have the appearance of being on the right side; among some of his more immediate friends, the economical plan of wearing two Faces under one Hat, has been introduced with striking effect."

Notwithstanding all the recent inventions, the True Blue on the Right side, and the good old English Fashion of wearing one face only, are and will be the prevailing Fashions in Banbury.

POTTS, PRINTER, ALBION OFFICE, BANBURY.

ABOVE LEFT: The present coat of arms shown on the Mayor's badge of office (The Charter Trustees).

RIGHT: Whig election poster.

BELOW LEFT: Corporation half gallon measure.

CORONER'S INQUEST.

An Inquest was held this Afternoon, at the Flying Horse Inn, before the Coroner and a respectable Jury, on the body of the Conservative Party, which died suddenly this Morning.

The Jury dispensed with the usual practice of viewing the body, which was reported to be in a very corrupt and offensive state: and after hearing the evidence, which was very conclusive, returned a Verdict of " *Felo-de-se.*"

Banbury, Tuesday, June 22, 1852.

POTTS AND SON, PRINTERS, PARSON'S STREET, BANBURY.

ABOVE: Banbury workhouse.

BELOW: Assumptions of mortality, 1852.

The Lying WHIGS

AT THEIR DIRTY WORK AGAIN.

These scoundrel Whigs have just sent forth a report that there are but two Candidates in the field.

There is another man **WHO WILL HEAD THE POLL** and his name is

Henry Vincent.

Vote for **HENRY VINCENT** *the only Reform Candidate and true friend of the people.*

Banbury, June, 28th, 1841.

CHENEY, PRINTER, BANBURY.

LEFT: In 1841, honest Henry tries hard, but
RIGHT: Henry William Tancred was Banbury's MP from 1832 to 1858.

BELOW: Banbury Town Seal, 1574.

John Stanbridge, master of St John's Hospital School in the early 16th
century, flanked by Blue Coat School pupils.

BELOW: Blue Coat School, housed in the gaol in the Market Place.

114

Learning the Lesson

See Jack in his study,
Is writing a book
As pretty as this is
In which you may look.
                          Rusher's Chap Book.

The first known school was that of St. John's Hospital and schoolmasters were first mentioned in 1345. It was made famous by its master, John Stanbridge, who taught there from 1501 until his death nine years later. He already had experience of Winchester, New College and Magdalen, and his teaching of grammar was renowned; he published several books including 'Accidence': a tract on eight parts of speech, supplemented by 'Gradus Comparationum' and 'Sum es fui', and 'Vocabula'—a vocabulary of Latin words for the body, trades, agriculture, etc. He had considerable success with his teaching and his example was followed by such noted schools as Manchester Grammar.

The other major school before the 19th century was the Blue Coat School founded by voluntary subscription in 1701 and supported by various legacies. High standards were demanded of the teachers:

'The schoolmaster is to be a member of the church of England, of a sober life and conversation, one that frequents the holy communion, one that has a good government of himself and his passions, of a meek temper, and humble behaviour; one who understands well the grounds and principles of the Christian religion, one who can write a good hand, and understands arithmetic, and shall be approved of by the minister. . . . The mistress to be qualified as the master (writing and arithmetic excepted), and to observe the same methods as the master, and to teach the girls to knit, sew mark and spin'. (Report of the Charity Commissioners 1826.)

The master earned £25 a year and the mistress £12.10s and if they accepted money from pupils or friends their jobs were forfeited. The children were provided with uniforms.

'Each boy to have a coat, breeches, cap, two bands, two shirts, two pairs of stockings, two pairs of shoes, and one pair of shoe buckles.

'Each girl to have two caps, two whiskes, one gown, one petticoat, two shifts, two pairs of stockings, one pair of knit gloves, two pairs of shoes, one pair of shoe buckles'. (Report of the Charity Commissioners 1826.)

The original school was in rooms over the Gaol in the market place, and when it opened education was provided for 30 boys and 20 girls. Rules were strict, but misbehaviour in church was common—for example:

'May 21, 1841 John Jones and Richd Taylor having been brought down and placed in the aisle of the church by the Sexton on Sunday last, for misbehaviour, the matter was brought before the meeting (of Trustees) and it was resolved that in future every Boy reported as behaving ill at church shall be immediately expelled'. (Blue Coat School Minute Book.)

After 1817 the Trustees paid £30 a year for the Blue Coat Children to attend the newly established Church of England National School. Masters at the National School received £75 a year and mistresses £50. By 1878 the school educated 212 boys and 161 girls in addition to the Blue Coat Children. Children were taught the usual 3Rs, and the girls earned money for the school with their needlework:

'The public are respectfully informed that Needlework and Knitting are done by the scholars . . . for Ready Money; and it is earnestly hoped that the reduction now made in the prices will obtain for the School a larger supply of work than theretofore.'

Items sewn included shirts for 1s 8d, nightcaps at 6d, stockings run at heel 3d, table cloths 2d and babies' caps 4d.

The school was supplemented by the Britannia Road School founded in 1860 and Christchurch School in South Banbury. The log book echoes the problem of attendance: 'May 16, 1894. In future, the class which makes the highest percentage of attendance during the week will receive a short time for play on Friday afternoon.'

The school did not try to compete with Banbury Fair—all the children were given a week off. The log book also accentuates the fact that children sometimes had short lives:

'May 13, 1907 Harold Thornton buried today. While climbing a tall tree on Ascension Day after a hawk's nest and when about half way up, he slipped, fell to the ground, and the poor lad broke his neck. The school sent a wreath and his class companions followed at the funeral.' (Christchurch Log Book.)

The Non-Conformists sent their children to British Schools—in 1839 Crouch Street British Schools was built and in 1861 Cherwell British Schools were provided by Bernhard Samuelson. Children came from outlying places such as Kings Sutton, Astrop, Adderbury, Bodicote, Shotteswell, Wroxton, Hanwell, Bloxham, Broughton, Edgehill and Moreton Pinkney. Some took lodgings in Banbury. The children were those of labourers, mechanics, small farmers and tradesmen. In addition to normal teaching, skills such as straw plaiting, needlework, knitting, darning, and mapping were taught to the girls, and mapping, drawing, geometry and mensuration to the boys.

These schools largely replaced the small dame schools of the early 19th century such as those attended by George Herbert:

'My earliest recollection is going to a dame school, her name was Kimberley. . . . I was then sent to school at Mr G. Claridge's . . . his school was two cottages made into one, but his school increased so much that he took the large building in the churchyard. It was a mixed school . . . the boys at one end of the room and the girls at the other.'

He then attended Mr Webster's school at Neithrop, which cost his father nine pence a week, plus money for books—at that time a small copybook cost 9d and a large one a shilling. This could be a large expense for parents.

The Banbury Municipal and Technical Day School was the first public secondary school in the town, founded with the help and encouragement of Bernhard Samuelson; when the idea was initiated in 1889 it was suggested that the headmaster, a graduate, should earn £350 and his science and art assistants £200. It aimed to provide commercial, technical and elementary education for boys of 13-17 who had passed Standard V exams. The building

116

adjoined the Mechanics Institute in Marlborough Road. The Mechanics Institute was set up in 1835 with the encouragement of Bernhard Samuelson, to provide adult education.

A series of historical accidents led to the establishment of Banbury School, which was destined to become the largest, and perhaps the best known comprehensive school in the country. Oxfordshire County Council purchased land adjacent to the grammar school and two secondary schools were built there in 1950s—one for girls and the other for boys. The idea of creating a large comprehensive school divided into several units emerged from a non-political debate in the 1960s. Pupils are taught in 'houses' on the collegiate model. Fortunately £300,000 was available for new buildings, and three units emerged for the 11-15 age group, and upper school.. The principal has overall responsibility, with independent heads for each hall. First principal was Harry Judge.

All Saints School, Bloxham was first founded 'for the Liberal Education of the Sons of the Clergy, Naval, Military and Professional Man and others, in 1853 by Rev John William Howett, who had come to the village the year before as an unpaid curate. He had to pretend he was affluent in order to open the school, although he only had £2,000, a library and some furniture, but despite this he had grandiose schemes to accommodate 140 pupils and build a quadrangle, library, oratory, chapel, porter's lodge, masters' apartments, ringing school, common room and dormitories. These plans exhausted his capital and after four years he was compelled to declare himself bankrupt and sell the school.

In 1860 the school was re-opened by Rev P. R. Egerton, curate of Deddington, who had seen the derelict school buildings and bought them. He was influenced by the aims of the Woodard Foundation, to give the children of the middle classes public school education with emphasis on the teachings of the Church of England. Egerton asked the Foundation to take the school under its wing, but was refused. His wife and her sisters helped to finance more building, and by 1896 it was well enough established to become part of the Woodard Foundation. Since then the school has increased in size, with far better buildings and facilities, and by 1960 had 260 pupils, the maximum figure intended.

LEFT: All Saints School, Bloxham.

RIGHT: Sunday School centenary tickets 1880
(Banbury Museum).

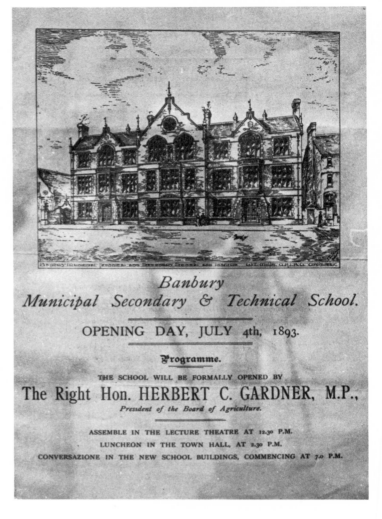

LEFT: Mechanics Institute lecture poster (Banbury Library).

ABOVE RIGHT: Programme commemorating the opening of Banbury Municipal Secondary and Technical School in 1893.

BELOW RIGHT: The Banbury Academy (Banbury Museum).

Fun and Games

Your doctor may sneer if he pleases,
But my recipe never will fail,
For the physic that cures all diseases
Is a bumper of Banbury ale.

May Day in Banbury has always had its own celebrations: maypoles were popular but suffered the same fate as the crosses. In 1589 Richard Wheatley, Constable of the Hundred of Banbury, ordered William Long, Constable of Neithrop and Calthorpe 'to take down all the maypoles within his district and to suppress and put down all Whitsun ales, May Games and morris dances and utterly to forbid any wakes or fairs to be kept'. People were furious and complaints were made to the Archbishop of Canterbury. Morris dancers survived and were popular until this century. Countrymen danced in the town and collected funds.

Bear and badger baiting were popular. Bear baiting took place in the bear garden outside West Bar, in the area once mistakenly thought to be a Roman amphitheatre. The animals were baited with dogs.

Many people participated in the various sports in the town. Banbury Harriers organised a great Whit Monday sports meeting early this century with 'champion walkers, runners and cyclists from all over the country taking part. Keepers of dancing bears, members of German bands and Italians with organs and monkeys' (John H. Langley). Wombwell's animals—an elephant and two fighting lions—were occasionally exhibited in Banbury.

Many sports clubs were started in Banbury—the Reindeer and the Three Tuns had bowling greens from the 16th century onwards, and in the 18th century the Reindeer had skittles. Quoits were popular—the Reindeer had a Quoits Club, as did The Plough. In 1891 the Chestnuts Bowling Club was formed; in 1832 the Cricket Club; 1875 the Football Club; 1876 the Bicycle Club. In 1879 the Central Exchange had a skating rink.

The Banbury Rugby Union Football Club celebrates its golden jubilee in 1975, having had an enthusiastic and successful first fifty years, during which time a clubhouse has been set up. All England Trial matches have been played in Banbury and a tour made to Dublin.

Banbury Races were notable events. The earliest recorded meeting at Banbury was on July 29, 1729, where the plate was £40, open to horses who had never won a stake worth 80 guineas. It was won by Mr Bertie's Lady Thigh. The 1738 meeting was a failure, with only two horses running for the £50 plate. After this races are not mentioned for nearly a century. In 1830 the Banbury Racing Club organised a day of three races. Only horses of modest pretensions were attracted. George Herbert mentions the races being held in Mill Meadows, and a horse called Brandy Nan, owned by Tommy Hartley, which won several

119

races. The new railways ran through Mill Meadows, and the races moved to Crouch Hill.

Many societies started in the 19th century—in 1858 The Archaeological Society was formed; in 1876 The Literary and Philosophical Society. Two notable ones in the 20th century are The Natural History Society and The Banbury Historical Society, both started in 1958.

The Banbury Horticultural Society and the Banbury Agricultural Society held annual shows in the 19th Century and greatly encouraged local gardeners.

Music flourished in the town—The Amateur Music Society performed monthly concerts from 1834 onwards and in 1844 was augmented by the Choral Society. The Banbury Philharmonic Society (1853) gave regular concerts in the National Schools, the Town Hall and the Central Corn Exchange. At the end of the century the Madrigal and Glee Union was initiated. Today the Music Society organises concerts.

The theatre has not been neglected. In 1768-80 new pieces performed by travelling companies included 'School for Scandal'. The earliest theatre in the Butchers' Shambles, was the Davenport. James Hill reconstructed it in Church Lane around 1832. It was brick, with boxes, a gallery and a pit. It could hold an audience of 200-300.

'It was used only by a theatrical manager named Jackman, who visited the town for three months every two years. On the night the Banbury Gas Company was inaugurated, Mr James Hill invited several gentlemen to a hot supper on the stage of his theatre, where it had been cooked by gas.' (Thomas Ward Boss).

The theatre closed in 1861 and subsequent companies performed in the Central Corn Exchange. The Banbury Cross Players, formed in 1947, perform plays and pantomimes in the town.

The first animated pictures were shown at the Central Corn Exchange by T. J. H. Blinkhorn, who in 1914 set up Blinkhorn's Picture House there. The Grand Cinema is now a bingo hall and the twin Classic cinemas provide a varied programme.

Queen Victoria visited Banbury Station twice, and was received by the Mayor and Corporation. On her second visit in 1869 both maces were carried in procession and the Queen was presented with a bunch of flowers and a box of Banbury cakes by Sarah Edith Harrison, the Mayor's daughter.

The other major entertainments were provided by Club Days, when children often played truant from school. Most Club Days were in July—the day started with clubs walking to the church in procession with bands and banners. Lunches were provided at each society's particular public house. Sports filled the afternoon, followed by more feasting, drinking and dancing.

The museum was established by the Mechanics Institute in the 19th century and until 1968 consisted of a few dusty showcases sandwiched between the Reading Room and the Reference Room in the Public Library. In 1968 it re-opened on the Second Floor, with help from the Oxford City & County Museum and the Department of Museum Studies, University of Leicester. The collections contain a wide variety of objects—from a 13th century crucifix from St. John's Hospital to the only known example of a Banbury cake basket made in Neithrop to a long case clock made by John Lamprey of Banbury and to a Victorian doll's house made for a local doctor's children. It also has a good collection of local photographs.

ABOVE: Banbury Football Club 1896-7 (Banbury Museum).

BELOW: Banbury Bowling Club (Banbury Museum).

121

ABOVE: Banbury Steeplechase, 1839.

BELOW LEFT: Frederick Charles Betts, who ran the Betts family cake business at 70 High Street. In his spare time he was an athlete, he belonged to the Banbury Harriers and won several medals (Mrs. Hughes).

BELOW RIGHT: Cricket Club threepenny token (Banbury Museum).

LEFT: Distin's Concert 1848 (Banbury Library).

RIGHT: Poster for Rob Roy, performed in the
Church Lane Theatre in 1823.

123

ABOVE: Queen Victoria's Diamond Jubilee,
1897—Grand celebration dinner.

BELOW: Spiceball Arts Centre, recently opened at The Mill.

Men of Moment

Ride a cock horse to Banbury Cross
To see what Emma can buy,
A penny white cake I'll buy for her sake
And a twopenny tart or pie.

Perhaps the individual who had most influence on 19th century Banbury was Sir Bernhard Samuelson—he fulfilled the role of patron which the Cope, Fiennes and North families had held. He changed the character of the town, in which he developed a strong economic interest. This was reflected in his parliamentary career, as Liberal Member of Parliament for Banbury in 1859 and 1865-1895. He had a particular interest in education, and in 1867 as chairman of the Royal Commission on Technical Education went on an educational tour of the continent, after which he made the following recommendation:

'Let no child under twelve be allowed to work until it can read and write. Make it the duty of every parent to see that its children have the means of elementary education. . . . Assist the pupils of elementary schools who have shown remarkable ability to continue their education in a superior school.'

Within three years an Act was passed making elementary education compulsory. He put his ideas into practice by building Cherwell British Schools, the Mechanics Institute and the Municipal Secondary School.

He played a prominent part in Banbury life; he was a member of the Board of Health, Governor of the Horton Infirmary, and supporter of the Banbury Agricultural Association. In 1905 he was created a Privy Councillor, and became Fellow of the Royal Society in recognition of his scientific achievements. Other honours included winning the Telford Medal in 1871 for a paper on the improvement of iron manufacture; in 1883-4 he was President of the Iron & Steel Institute; in 1878 he was a member of the Royal Commission on the Paris Exhibition; in 1886 Chairman of the Associated Chambers of Commerce and a member of the Vigilance Committee of the British Iron Trade Association. He was the first President of the Association of Agricultural Engineers, Justice of the Peace and Alderman of Oxfordshire County Council.

In 1844 he married Caroline Blundell of Hull, and had five sons and seven daughters. Three years after Caroline's death in 1886 he married Celia, widow of William Denny. He died in 1905.

Then again, Thomas Colley, a local baker, nicknamed the Banbury Pedestrian, in 1816 accepted a wager that he could walk 1020 miles in 20 successive days, which he did between 20 March and 8 April:

'The Pedestrian was then Chaired down and up the Course, amidst the Acclamations and

Congratulations of many Thousand Spectators, who assembled to witness the Completion of this Arduous Undertaking. . . . He was next day taken round the Town in a Chaise and Four, and afterwards Chaired in triumph, attended with many Flags, and a large Concourse of Spectators. An Ox was roasted in the Field, on the Day of the Performance.' (Statement issued to Subscribers).

The walk aroused considerable interest in the town—Sarah Beesley recalls that at the age of four she was taken by her nursemaid to watch the Pedestrian at five o'clock in the morning. Although he fulfilled the wager, he died shortly afterwards as a result of his exertions.

One notorious character was 'Old Parr', who murdered Lydia Wild, a slatter's widow, on March 7, 1746-7. The Oxford Flying Weekly Journal reported that she was found 'barbarously murdered in her own kitchen; there were several wounds upon her head, one of which is very large and appears to have been done with a hammer, and her throat was cut almost from ear to ear'. Parr was an Irish plush weaver, who was discovered with his clothes and boots covered with blood. He was tried, convicted and hanged in Horsefair before being gibbeted on 'Parr's Piece' near Easington Farm. Beesley tells us:

'It is said that Parr's body fell from the gibbet . . . and that some chimneysweepers thereupon made a procession with the body through the town . . .'.

The story was long used to terrorise Banbury children, and early this century Old Parr's ghost was "seen" a number of times—as Rev Mead, vicar of Christchurch, was walking home up Old Parr Road at 2.30 one morning he saw a little man before him; as he approached, the figure walked into the bank and disappeared; the figure was clad in a fustian jacket, with cord trousers tied at the knee, a billycock hat and a red kerchief. Mr Pitcher, who related the story to me, went with his brother to search for the ghost, but they found nothing. Their mother once saw him—a little figure smoking a pipe, who said nothing when she bid him 'Good Morning'. She ran home in terror. After the ghost had been seen several times on the vicarage lawn, Rev Mead concluded that the spirit could not rest in peace, and the next time he saw it he made the sign of the cross and said 'Enter and rest in peace', and the ghost was never seen again.

Another long remembered murder was that of John Kalabergo, an Italian jeweller, watchmaker and optician who had a shop in the Market Place. He went back to Italy in 1850 and brought his nephew back to help in the shop. The nephew was impetuous and they quarrelled. One day in 1852 Kalabergo and his nephew drove out to visit clients in the Priors Marston district. Thomas Ward Boss describes the evening events;

'That evening between five and six o'clock some persons saw the horse and trap standing in the road with no-one in charge. They led the horse towards Williamscote and about half way up the hill found the body of Mr Kalabergo in a pool of blood on the ice and snow. The corpse was taken to the Inn at Williamscote, and the cart brought to Banbury. Soon after six o'clock the nephew called on the Rev T. Tandy, the Roman Catholic priest, to whom he told a rambling story that he and his uncle had been attacked by robbers, that he had escaped through the hedge, and guided by the lights, made his way across the fields to Banbury, leaving his uncle much injured. Notwithstanding this story, he was arrested the same night and in a few days committed to Oxford for wilful murder. It was some weeks before the pistol was found (supposed to be in consequence of a dream) in a watercourse between Williamscote Hill and the turnpike road, over which the murderer had run. The evidence was very conclusive, he was tried at the Lent Assizes, and in a few weeks hanged at Oxford. A few friends of the late John Kalabergo erected a memorial stone to their highly esteemed townsman on Williamscote Hill'. (This stone is now in Banbury Museum).

'Old Mettle' enlivened Banbury life in the 19th century. His real name was William Castle, and he was born about 1789 of an Adderbury family. As a child he had an accident which deformed his legs so that he was unable to do steady work:

'. . . he had a way of living by his wits . . . he might amuse the gaping crowds around him by playing the fool . . . so long and so well did Mettle ape the fool that most persons considered him . . . as really being a fool'. (Banbury Pamphlets p.94).

He earned his living as a carver and gilder and as a sulphur match seller. When people told him he was a fool, he would reply that there was a fool in every family, but it was his brother who was the fool, for he went to work. Because he acted the fool Mettle was bombarded with free tobacco and drinks. He often wore strange clothes:

'Mettle's favourite dress was of the oddest patchwork sort that he could put together. Sometimes he wore a huge cocked hat like a beadle. On another occasion, a straw hat or bonnet of enormous dimensions, which some . . . English lady had brought from Paris. On two occasions, and two only, he assumed a graver garb. In one instance some wag of the University of Oxford gave him a cap and gown, in which Mettle did not fail to go about, and in which he stood for his portrait to Mr Levy. . . . The other instance of Mettle's gravity was when his mother died. The poor fellow, who was a diligent church-goer, thought it right on that occasion to appear like other people; so he begged a common hat a common coat, waistcoat, and trousers, all of a rusty black, a white shirt, and, for a time, looked almost like a gentleman'. (Banbury Pamphlets pp. 94-95).

He played a part in the political life of the town. The radicals of Banbury put him forward as the candidate in opposition to the Guilford interest, and he stood for all the elections between 1818-31. The 'ladies of the Banbury Rads' made him favours from deal shavings. He was a popular candidate, and though never elected, was always chaired round the town. The Reform Bill gave votes to Mettle's radical supporters, so his faction rapidly declined.

Mettle was once charged at Oxford, of having been concerned with others in a burglary at Neithrop. His efforts to play the fool in court were of no avail, and he was sentenced to be hanged, but his friends got up a petition stating that he was generally considered to be an idiot, and he was pardoned. He continued to parade the streets, and act as fool for the morris dancers until his sudden death in June 1841 of an apoplexy. He was remembered in Banbury a long time.

The first 'History of Banbury' was written by Alfred Beesley including copious historical and antiquarian notes of the neighbourhood. He was born in 1800 and served as apprentice to a Deddington watchmaker, giving up this profession in favour of literary and scientific pursuits. His history of the town was published in parts by subscriptions and he appealed to the public for support. The book was duly published in 1841. He died in 1847.

William Potts, (1868-1947) wrote a thoroughly researched book on the history of the town, which, owing to paper shortage during the war, was not published until 1958, eleven years after his death. It was edited by Mr E. T. Clark, then editor of the Banbury Guardian. He also wrote 'Banbury in Coaching Days', 'Banbury Cross and the Rhyme', 'Banbury through 100 years' and 'The Story of Banbury Church'.

George Herbert wrote a somewhat different book about Banbury. He was born in 1814, the son of a plush weaver. He became a shoemaker, but despite his hard work, bad debtors made him bankrupt, so he changed his trade to photography. His book 'Shoemaker's

'Window' is a fascinating collection of reminiscences of Banbury before the railway age.

The magisterial Volume 10 of the *Victoria County History of Oxfordshire* consists chiefly of an authoritative, documented history of Banbury and is unusual for being mainly based upon the researches of local scholars—W. C. Braithwaite, E. R. C. Brinkworth, J. S. W. Gibson, R. K. Gilkes, B. S. Trinder.

For more than 100 years two newspapers, founded by local men, have conveyed the news to the inhabitants. The first of these was founded in 1838—The Guardian. Its sole purpose was to diffuse 'information respecting the new Poor Law' and, by providing an impartial record of the proceedings of the Board of Guardians, newly established, prevent 'wild and foolish reports'.

The paper's founder was William Potts (grandfather of the historian), a printer of Parson's Street, who had come to the town from Daventry. 'The Guardian', published monthly, met with immediate success. Gradually more general news appeared in its columns. Potts was pressed to found a weekly paper and on July 4, 1843, in his Mayoral year, he produced the first edition of 'The Banbury Guardian'.

William Potts was succeeded by his son, John, who appointed local correspondents in the villages and he produced the first Times size eight page editions. In 1892 he was succeeded by his son, William, who introduced mechanical typesetting. He also started the 'Banbury Evening News' as a result of a dispute with the Post Office but this paper was not continued for long.

Before his death William Potts established a company to carry on the newspaper. Arthur Butler edited the paper for a few years and was followed by E. T. Clark into the early 1960s. The paper was eventually taken over by the Woodrow Wyatt group and shortly after by the Courier Press (Holdings) Ltd.

'The Banbury Advertiser' was founded in 1854 by George Walford who published it from 72 High Street and the family controlled it for sixty years until Benjamin Morland bought it and from his Gatteridge Street works published a series covering also Brackley and Chipping Norton. On Benjamin Morland's death a company was formed with C. Randolph Webb and William Henry Russell as directors. The latter was unfortunately killed in a motor accident. The paper also came into the hands of Courier Press (Holdings) Ltd. but shortly afterwards, they ceased publication.

LEFT: Sir Bernhard Samuelson, MP.

RIGHT: Theodore Lamb, a Sibford man who became a hermit, supposedly after being crossed in love.

ABOVE AND BELOW: The Banbury Pedestrian
and his walking stick (Banbury Museum).

RIGHT: Old Mettle in academic dress and in his straw hat and curls.

The Banbury Pedestrian, ----- Thomas Colley;

Started to perform 1020 Miles in 20 successive Days, near Banbury.

First Day, WEDNESDAY, 20th March, 1816, at ¼ past 5 o'Clock, A.M., in good Spirits: went 20 Miles before Breakfast, 31 Miles before Dinner, and at ½ past 8 o'Clock P.M. performed 53 Miles.

2nd Day, Thursday, 21st March, Started ¼ past 5 o'clock. In the Evening, Drum and Fife paraded near the Lines of the Course. Performed this Day 47 Miles, at ½ past 9 o'clock. Wet Night.

3rd Day, Friday, 22nd March, Started after 6 o'clock, in good Spirits. But, in consequence of its being a very Wet Day, and the Course very slippery, (not being sufficiently prepared for the bad Weather,) he performed only 41 Miles.

4th Day, Saturday, 23rd March, Started about 5 o'clock, in very good Spirits. Rain about an Hour. Performed this Day 52 Miles, about 9 o'clock. Great Drum, and Drum and Fife, paraded near the Course in the Evening.

5th Day, Sunday, 24th March, Started before 4 o'clock. Stopped during Divine Service. Performed 52 Miles, before 11 o'clock, P.M.

6th Day, Monday, 25th March, Started ¼ before 5 o'clock; performed 51 Miles, about 10 o'clock.

7th Day, Tuesday, 26th March, Started after 4 o'clock, and at ½ past 10 o'clock performed 53 Miles.

8th Day, Wednesday, 27th March, Started ¼ before 5 o'clock, in good Spirits, and performed 52 Miles, before 11 o'clock.

9th Day, Thursday, 28th March, Started at 5 o'clock, and performed 51 Miles, after 8 o'clock.

10th Day, Friday, 29th March, Started after 4 o'clock, and about 11 o'clock, performed 56 Miles.

11th Day, Saturday, 30th March, Started about ½ past 4 o'clock, and performed 52 Miles, before 11 o'clock.

12th Day, Sunday, 31st March, Started at 4 o'clock, and performed 52 Miles, at ¼ before 11 o'clock.

13th Day, Monday, 1st April, Started after 4 o'clock, and performed 47½ Miles before 10 o'clock.

14th Day, Tuesday, 2nd April, Started at ¼ past 3 o'clock, and performed 53½ Miles after 10 o'clock.

15th Day, Wednesday, 3rd April, Started after 4 o'clock, A.M., and performed 53 Miles, at about ¼ after 10 o'clock, P.M.

16th Day, Thursday, 4th April, Started at ½ past 4 o'clock, and performed 53 Miles, at about ½ past 10 o'clock.

17th Day, Friday, 5th April, Started before 5 o'clock, and performed 51 Miles, at 11 o'clock.

18th Day, Saturday, 6th April, Started after 4 o'clock, and performed 51 Miles, after 10 o'clock.

19th Day, Sunday, 7th April, Started about ½ past 3 o'clock, and performed 53½ Miles, before 12 o'clock.

20th Day, Monday, 8th April, Started after 3 o'clock, A.M., and performed 41½ Miles, before 7 o'clock P.M., when he completed 1021 Miles in the 20 Days.

The Pedestrian was then Chaired down and up the Course, amidst the Acclamations and Congratulations of many Thousand Spectators, who assembled to witness the completion of this arduous Undertaking, when he retired to rest. He was the next day taken round the Town in a Chaise and Four, and afterwards Chaired, in triumph, attended with many Flags, and a large Concourse of Spectators.

An Ox was Roasted in the Field, on the last Day of the Performance.

To complete the Distance of 1021 Miles, he daily walked many times to and from the place of Repose to the Starting-Post, &c., making together more than 5 Miles.

☞ THIS STATEMENT IS GIVEN ONLY TO SUBSCRIBERS.

Colley's itinerary.

ABOVE LEFT AND RIGHT: John Kalabergo, and his
shop in the Market Place.

BELOW RIGHT: Kalabergo's nephew and murderer and LEFT:
the site of the murder on Williamscote Hill (Banbury Museum).

131

ABOVE: Newspaper advertisement about the Kalabergo trial (Cheneys). BELOW: A Banbury murder (Cheneys).

LEFT: 1884 edition of the Banbury Guardian and
CENTRE: An advertisement for the Banbury Guardian
(Banbury Museum).

ABOVE RIGHT: Alfred Beesley, author of the town's
first history (Banbury Museum).

BELOW RIGHT: William Potts, founder of the
Banbury Guardian (E. T. Clark).

133

ABOVE: A last look at the past—Green and Horsefair c. 1850.

LEFT: A bust of Shakespeare marks the site of the
Shakespeare tavern and Registry for servants.

BELOW: The museum and library bridge old and new Banbury.

134

Banbury Today

Ride a cock horse to Banbury Cross,
To see a fine lady on a white horse,
With rings on her fingers and bells on her toes,
Who can't find her way in a one way street.

Heard on BBC Radio 4

The dust has now settled since the demolition of the near-derelict brick buildings north of the Market Place, making way for a new central area development. Modern buildings are beginning to rise and the population has begun to discern the future shape of the town.

Banbury's change from a small market town, dependent on agriculture and the remains of the iron and weaving industries, began in 1929. Samuelson's Britannia Works was on the decline. Henry Stone & Son's box file factory had increased its production and diversified into photo-engraving and colour printing; Cheney's, Banbury's oldest business, had recovered from the fire which destroyed their works in 1923 and Spencer Corsets Ltd. had opened in Britannia Road. These industries were not major employers. Countrywide unemployment was brought home forcibly when Scottish hunger marchers stopped in the town for the night on their sad way to London early in 1930.

At the time the Northern Aluminium Company was looking for a site on which to build a rolling mill. George Oakes, Borough Accountant, Arthur Stockton, Town Clerk and Alderman John Collingridge, Mayor in 1928, opened negotiations with the firm and also with Alderman W. I. R. Lidsey, a former Mayor, for part of the land the latter farmed at Hardwick and which adjoined the Southam Road. Negotiations continued over many weeks, mainly on the question of price. There was a difference of £2,000 between the figure the company would pay and that which Lidsey would accept.

When the town council met in emergency session members were told that to bridge the gap Mr and Mrs Joseph Gillett had offered a gift of £500 and had secured a further gift of £500 from a relative, the company would pay £200 more. So members of the council individually guaranteed the balance between them. The agreement was signed April 1 1930 and the new mill came into production November 1931. In 1930 the County School, so long housed in Marlborough Road, moved to new premises at Easington. Neithrop House was opened as a clinic and plans made for the extension of the People's Park into the grounds of the house. In July the Red Lion coaching inn in the High Street was demolished to make way for Woolworths store. In November of the following year cattle were sold in the streets of the town for the last time, the Town Council having rented a portion of the saleyard Midland Marts had built just beyond the bridge in 1925, for a dealers' market. The Midland Marts cattle market has become the biggest cattle market in Europe.

With the arrival of the aluminium producing plant the provision of housing and ancillary services assumed urgent importance. Housing efforts had previously been confined to slum clearance and replacement, principally at Easington, Neithrop and Grimsbury. In January 1933, 160 council houses were formally opened by the Mayor, Councillor James Friswell, at Ruscote. Near the railway, where the sidings had been largely extended in 1930 to cope with expected new traffic, a new postal sorting office was opened. New sewage works were commenced in 1934. A telephone building was put up behind the Post Office in the High Street and an automatic exchange installed in 1935 and the frontage of the Post Office rebuilt. A new Police Station was opened in December 1935. A water scheme was begun in 1936. By September 1939 the population of the town had grown to 19,000.

In the late 1930s British Nylon Spinners had purchased 86 acres of land on the Southam Road at Banbury for a factory. However, under government decree, they had been forced to build in South Wales, an area at that time under economic stress. Permission had been given for industrial building on the Banbury land. The borough council, anxious to introduce a diversity of industry after the war, in 1952 asked British Nylon Spinners if they intended to build at Banbury. They said no and offered to sell to the council. Banbury purchased the 86 acres for £41,000.

Oxfordshire planning authority then pointed out to Banbury that if industry was to be expanded a new Town Map would be necessary. Somewhat hesitantly the council agreed to an expansion from 20,000 to 40,000. They proceeded to sign 'overspill' agreements to accept and house population under the 1952 Town Development Act. These agreements were with the Greater London Council and with Birmingham County Borough Council. In the latter case the agreement was limited to facilitate the removal to Banbury in the early 1960s of the giant Birds Foods concern who were to build on the Southam Road land.

In May 1961 the council invited the Civic Trust to prepare a scheme for the remodelling of the central area to cope with the proposed expansion. In the autumn of 1962 a special meeting of the council was called to consider a sixth and 'final' report by the Trust. Briefly, this plan, called 3D, proposed the demolition and redevelopment of the whole of the area north of the Market Place from the eastern end of Parson's Street to the existing realigned Castle Street bordering the new bus station. Forty shops were to be demolished as well as the Town Hall and ninety shops were to be built. A relief road from a realigned Castle Street, across Bridge Street to the junction of George Street and Broad Street defined the easterly limits of the town centre. Inside the ring road were to be pedestrian precincts.

While this was still keenly debated locally, Bird's negotiations with the borough council for a factory site were closing. They signed the contract in January 1963. More than 100 possible sites throughout the United Kingdom had been investigated and the final choice had fallen on Banbury.

The ink expended on plan 3D was hardly dry when, in 1964, the Ministry of Housing and Local Government published the 'South-East Study 1961-81'. This showed a New Town on the edge of Banbury to the east. Banbury was suddenly and unexpectedly faced with the alternative of expanding beyond 40,000 or being dwarfed by a New Town. Borough councillors agreed to enter into a feasibility study for expanding the town to 70,000 'without obligation'.

The resulting plan produced by the Oxfordshire County Council with Ministerial approval, envisaged a central area with some of the surrounding villages converted to small satellite towns. The final decision rested on the will of Banbury people.

The plan was debated at a special meeting of the borough council, with members of Banbury Rural District Council, officials of the Ministry of Housing and Local Government, Board of Trade, Greater London Council, Oxfordshire County Council, consultants and officials. It was also publicly debated at a packed, lively meeting at the Town Hall in November.

Most were against the plan. They were concerned about the loss of the traditional town; farmers were troubled about lost acres, villagers of village atmosphere, shopkeepers about compensation and new rents and there was no guidance as to whether the town could expect a by-pass or an enlarged hospital.

The matter had also become political. In general, the Labour party was in favour of expansion for more employment opportunities and better services; the Conservatives, against. The council was equally divided between the Labour and Conservative parties, met to take a decision, and the votes were equal. The Mayor gave his casting vote—against. The following year the County Council was asked to review the Town Map on the basis of a population of 41,000 in 1981 and prepare a town centre map.

About this time developers had purchased the Elizabethan Original Cake Shop in Parson's Street, the property adjoining, on the corner of Church Lane, and a block of property behind, fronting the Lane. The famous Banbury Cakes had been sold from the shop for 200 years or so. One morning the town was alerted when they saw workmen stripping the roof of the shop. Representations were immediately made to the workmen and to the planning authorities in Oxford and London. A stop was ordered and battle joined to save the building. But demolition had gone too far.

As in previous plans, the proposals put forward in 1969 faced up to the traffic threat. The Town Centre Map envisages a central shopping core largely free of vehicles, the removal of through traffic, the provision of adequate car parking around the ring and the development of the area north of the Market Place for an extension of the shopping area, linked to the Market Place by pedestrian ways.

A comprehensive redevelopment of the George Street area, covering 21 acres and including the 'Brewery site' is envisaged for parking and business premises, although proposals are not in a detailed state. The waterside area, north of Bridge Street including Spiceball Park, is seen as an important amenity. Distributor traffic roads are planned to exclude traffic from the central area and of immense importance to the town's future is the prospect of a north-south motorway, or Banbury by-pass, still subject to debate at Government level.

While these various schemes for the town's future were undergoing intense examination the development of the Southam Road industrial area was proceeding at an accelerating pace. Automotive Products were the first to build and they were followed by Bird's which, in 1947, had become part of the American owned General Foods Corporation international division. Seventeen firms, many with 'household' names have now established themselves there. In 1971 a new site for industrial development was commenced on the Daventry Road and this came into operation in 1973. Smaller sites in the Cherwell Street area and on the Overthorpe Road have also been developed.

One of the later major decisions taken by the borough council before re-organisation into the Cherwell District on March 31, 1974, was the provision of a Leisure Centre at Spiceball Park.

When the 1973 census was taken Banbury's population was 31,060, approximately 17,000 greater than at the start of its industrial development forty-three years before.

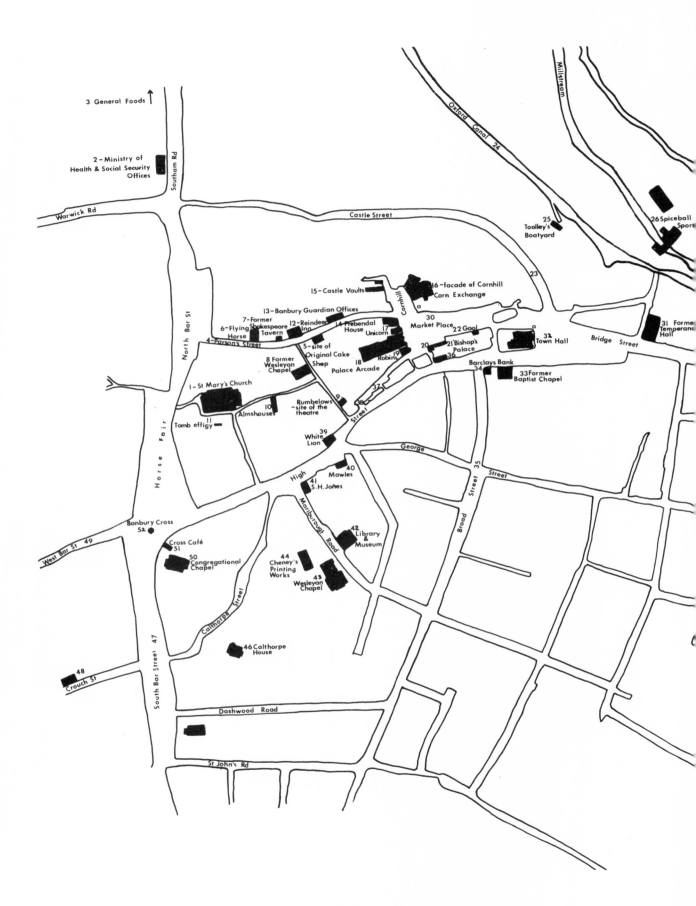

3 General Foods ↑

2 - Ministry of
Health & Social Security
Offices

Southam Rd

Warwick Rd

Castle Street

Oxford Canal 24

Millstream

25 Toolley's
Boatyard

26 Spiceball Sport

23

15 - Castle Vaults

16 - facade of Cornhill
Corn Exchange

Cornhill

a

13 - Banbury Guardian Offices

30 Market Place

31 Former
Temperance Hall

Bridge Street

North Bar St

7 - Former
Shakespeare Tavern

6 - Flying
Horse

12 - Reindeer Inn

14 Prebendal
House

17 Unicorn

22 Gaol

a

32 Town Hall

4 - Parson's Street

5 - site of
Original Cake Shop

20

21 'Bishop's
Palace

36

8 Former
Wesleyan
Chapel

18 Palace Arcade

19 Robins

Barclays Bank

34

33 Former
Baptist Chapel

1 - St Mary's Church

Street

37

Horse Fair

10 Almshouses

Rumbelows
- site of the
theatre

9

38

11 Tomb effigy

39 White Lion

George Street

40 Mawles

Broad Street 35

Marlborough Road

High Street

41 S.H.Jones

Banbury Cross
52

West Bar St 49

Cross Café
51

42 Library
& Museum

50 Congregational
Chapel

44 Cheney's
Printing Works

43 Wesleyan
Chapel

Calthorpe Street

46 Calthorpe
House

South Bar Street 47

48
Crouch St

Dashwood Road

St John's Rd

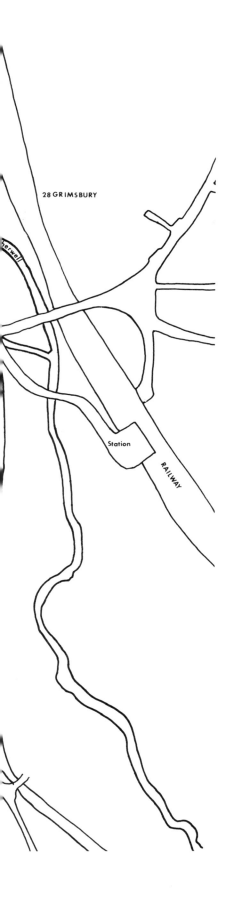

28 GRIMSBURY

Station

RAILWAY

Crispin Paine designed this walk through Banbury's past.

1. St Mary's Church, built in 1790, and described by the Gentleman's Magazine as 'more like a gaol than a Christian temple.' 2. 'The Kremlin'—new Social Security Offices. 3. The green block in the distance is the General Foods factory. 4. Parson's Street is apparently so called because so many houses in it were owned by the church. It contains a variety of buildings in local stone, brick and timber frame. 5. The site of the Original Cake Shop. 6. The Flying Horse was the headquarters of the local Liberal party in the 19th century. 7. The bust of Shakespeare marks the site of the Shakespeare Tavern. 8. Former Wesleyan Chapel. 9. The site of the Davenport Theatre, in use from about 1830 until 1861. 10. Almshouses. Formerly a large number of buildings, including a tithe barn were clustered around the church. 11. A decayed tomb effigy removed from the old church. 12. The Reindeer Inn, partly dating from the early 16th century. In Charles I's reign the Globe Room was added at the back. 13. Offices of the Banbury Guardian, founded in 1838. 14. Prebendal House, a much restored 17th century building. 15. The Castle Vaults and house attached, designed by William Wilkinson. 16. Façade of the Cornhill Corn Exchange. 17. 17-19 Market Place, built as the Unicorn Inn in 1648. 18. The Palace Arcade, the other corn exchange which became Banbury's first cinema. 19. Robins Brothers—an interesting timber framed building with pargetting. 20. Kettering and Leicesters, another 17th century building. 21. 'The Bishop's Palace' has a plastered timber front and a stone back. 22. Gordon Jarvis bookmakers—this building was built by the Corporation about 1610 as a wool market, and used as a gaol from 1646-1852, and housed the Blue Coat School above the Gaol. 23. Castle Street once led to the castle gate. Nothing remains above ground of the castle. 24. The Oxford Canal, designed by James Brindley. 25. Herbert Tooley's boatyard, which has an 18th century dry dock. 26. Spiceball Arts and Sports Centre. 27. The bridge over the mill stream conceals the 13th century arches. 28. Grimsbury became a Victorian working class suburb. It now includes Midland Marts, one of Europe's largest cattle markets. 29. Chapman Brothers' warehouse was once the old town hall, removed here in 1860. 31. The Temperance Hall, built in 1875. 32. The Town Hall, designed by E. Bruton in 1854. 33. The former Baptist Chapel has now been converted to form part of Fine Fare. 34. Barclays Bank, once Gillett's New Bank, founded in 1784 and bought in 1822 by the plush manufacturer, Joseph Ashby Gillett. 35. Broad Street leads to the site of Cole Bar and Newland. 36. 85-87 High Street, built in 1650 by Edward Vivers, a woollen draper and leading local Quaker. The back of the building is of stone. 37. Butchers' Row is typical of the narrow lanes which grew out of market stalls. 38. Site of the Bread Cross. 39. The White Lion, a prominent coaching inn. 40. Mawles' has a fascinating façade. 41. S. H. Jones and Sons, a much restored house of 1537. 42. The building which houses the Library and Museum was originally The Mechanics Institute and Municipal School. 43. Wesleyan Chapel. 44. Cheney and Sons, printers. This business was founded around 1767. 45. The Catholic Church, built in 1838. 46. Calthorpe House, built in 16th century. It has been used as a house, a cloth factory, a girls' school, and is now offices and flats. 47. South Bar was once *the* place to live in Banbury. 48. Gothic stucco houses in Crouch Street. 49. West Bar was built up in the 1860s and 70s with middle class houses in the North Oxford style. 50. Congregational Chapel, built in Doric style. 51. Cross Cafe, typical of the stone houses which once comprised most of the town. 52. Banbury Cross was erected to commemorate the marriage of the Princess Royal to the Crown Prince of Prussia in 1858. The statues of Queen Victoria, Edward VII and George V were added in 1914.

139

ABOVE : A crane dominates the town, emphasising
Banbury's future shopping centre.

CENTRE : A desolate site lies behind Banbury's old facades.

BELOW : Skeletal steelwork marks the future sports complex.

140

ABOVE : New shops invade Parson's Street.

RIGHT : Progress reaches out for a period
survivor, Prebendal House.

ABOVE RIGHT: As heirs to the Samuelson tradition, Alcan's factory lies behind the canal while

BELOW RIGHT: Those in need have nicknamed the new Social Security building The Kremlin.

ABOVE LEFT: The town's industrial élite is assured with the North Oxford Technical College and

BELOW LEFT: New shops bring new life to Church Walk.

Banbury's future is perhaps summarised by the largest local employer,
General Foods. (ABOVE); continuing commercial development as in
Warwick Road (CENTRE); and with the emphasis on education at the
School of Art (BELOW).

143

Bibliography

Allison, K. J., Beresford, M. W., Hurst J. G., etc.; The Deserted Villages of Oxfordshire, Dept. of English Local History, Occasional Papers No. 17; Leicester University Press 1966.
also; The Deserted Villages of Northamptonshire, Paper No. 18.
Aplin R., Reminiscences of Banbury—oral communication.
Arthur Jonas 'Harvest of the Fields' manuscript lent to Banbury Museum.
also; A Cherwell Boy—manuscript lent to Banbury Museum.
Baker M.—Discovering English fairs.
Banbury Cuttings—Bound scrapbook, largely consisting of press-cuttings and posters in Banbury Reference Library.
Barratt D. M. and Vaisey D. G.—Oxfordshire; A Handbook for Students of Local History—Basil Blackwell 1973.
Barrett G.—Letter to Thomas Boss May 16/17 1900—Typescript in Potts collection 990.71.329.
Beckinsale R. P.—The Plush Industry of Oxfordshire—Oxonierisia Vol. XXXVIII 1963.
Beesley A.—History of Banbury, London 1841.
Beesley Sarah—My Life, Banbury 1892.
Boss Thomas Ward—Reminiscences of Old Banbury 1903 Wm. Potts.
Bowen C. J.—The Hospitaller Knights of St. John of Jerusalem—Art & Book Co., London & Leamington 1894.
Braithwaite Wm. C.—Banbury: the town and village community in the middle ages. Banbury Guardian Offices 1913.
Briggs Katharine M.—The Folklore of the Cotswolds—Batsford 1974.
Bromley V.—Roman Banburyshire—Cake & Cockhorse Vol. 2, No. 7, Jan. 1964.
Cake & Cockhorse, Journal of Banbury Historical Society.
Cheke, Val.—The Story of Cheese-making in Britain—Routledge and Kegan Paul 1959.
Cheney C. R.—Cheney & Sons: Two centuries of printing in Banbury—Cake & Cockhorse Vol. III, No. 9, Autumn 1967.
Cheney C. R.—Early Banbury chapbooks and broadsides (The Library, 1937, SW4, Vol. 17, pp. 98-108).
Claridge, John—The Shepherd of Banbury's Rules to judge of the changes of the weather, grounded on 40 years experience. Printed for W. Bickerton, London 1744.
Coleman S. Jackson—Oracles of Oxon.
Darby H. C. and Terrett, I. R.—The Domesday Geography of Midland England. Cambridge University Press 1954.
Everitt A.—'The Primary Towns of England'; Local Historian Vol. II, No. 5, Feb. 1975, pp. 268-277.
Flick, Pauline—The Rollright Stones—A problem of Conservation—Country Life, August 30 1973, pp. 560-1.
General Foods—The Food Makers, 1972.
Gibson, J. S. W.—Traveller's Tales Part I—Cake & Cockhorse, Vol. V, No. 7, pp. 127-139.
Harrison B. and Trinder, B.—Drink and Sobriety in an Early Victorian Country Town: Banbury 1830-1860—English Historical Review, Supplement 4—Longmans 1969.
Harvey, P. D. A.—Where was Banbury Cross? Oxoniensia XXXI.
Herbert, George—Shoemaker's Window, Phillimore 1971.
Historic Towns: Banbury; Lovell, Johns, Cook, Hammond & Kell Organisation.
Hoskins, W. G.—Fieldwork in Local History; Faber 1967.
Johnson, William Ponsonby—The History of Banbury and its Neighbourhood; C. Walford, Banbury; c. 1865.
Laithwaite, Michael—Cake Horse Vol. 2, No. 10, November, 1964.
Langley, John H.—Further Memories of late Victorian and Early Edwardian Banbury—Cake & Cockhorse Vol. III, No. 2, Spring 1966 pp. 43-44.
MacNamara, F. M.—Memorials of the Danvers Family; Hardy & Page, London 1895.
Martin, A. F. and Steel, R. W., ed.—The Oxford Region; The Oxford University Press, 1954.
May, Jeffrey—Excavations at Madmarston, Ncrth Oxfordshire—Interim Report.
Opie, Iona and Peter, ed.—The Oxfordshire Dictionary of Nursery Rhymes; Oxford University Press, 1951.
Ordnance Survey—Map of Monastic Britian South Sheet—2nd edition, 1954 H.M.S.O.
also Map of Roman Britain—3rd edition, 1956 H.M.S.O.
Orme Nicholas—English Schools in the Middle Ages; Methuen & Co. Ltd., 1973.
Pearson, Edwin—Banbury Chap Books and Nursery Toybook Literature of the 18th and early 19th centuries; London 1890.
Plot, R.—Natural History of Oxfordshire—1677.
Potts, William—A History of Banbury; Banbury 1958.
Potts, William—Manuscript Notes in Banbury Museum.
Potts, William—Banbury Cross and The Rhyme; Banbury 1930.
Potts, William—Banbury Through 100 Years; Banbury 1942.
Potts, William—Banbury In The Coaching Days; Banbury 1929.
Radford, E. and M. A.—Encyclopaedia of Superstitions—Book Club Associates 1974.
Rolt, L. T. C.—Narrow Boat; Eyre & Spottiswoode, 1944.
Saunders, Ian—Thenford Roman Villa; Typescript.
Steane, John M.—The Northamptonshire Landscape; Hodder & Stoughton, 1974.
Sherwood, J. and Pevsner, N.—Oxfordshire; Penguin Books, 1974.
Sutton, J. E. G.—Iron Age Hill-forts and some other Earthworks in Oxfordshire—Oxoniensia. XXXI (1966), pp. 28-43.
Townshend, James, M.A.—The Oxfordshire Dashwoods; Private Circulation OUP 1922.
Toynbee Margaret and Young, Peter—Cropredy Bridge 1644—The Campaign and the Battle; Roundwood Press 1970.
Victoria County History of Oxford, Vol. I, ed. William Page—published Archibald Constable, London 1907; (contributors: ecclesiastical—Rev. H. E. Salter, M.A.; Social & Education—Miss Beatrice A. Lees; Population—George S. Minchin; Industries— Reginald W. Jeffery M.A.; Racing—Capt. P. H. M. Wynter).
Victoria County History; Vol. IX & X.
Views & Reviews—Banbury Special Edition; pub. by W. T. Pike & Co., Brighton, 1897.
Wood, Jones R. S. S.—Traditional Domestic Architecture of the Banbury Region; Manchester University Press, 1963.
Woods, K. S. — Rural Industries Round Oxford 1921.
Young, Peter—Edgehill 1642—The Campaign and the Battle; The Roundwood Press, 1967.

Index

Subscribers

Presentation copies

1 **LORD SAYE AND SELE**
2 **The Charter Trustees**
3 **Banbury Library**
4 **Banbury Museum**
5 **Cherwell District Council**

6 Christine Bloxham
7 Clive Birch
8 John Portergill
9 J. H. Fearon
10 Lord Saye and Sele
11 John Bloxham
12 Herr Bent Ivensen
13 Alan Jones
14 Frü Svea Sandberg
15 Capt. John Lovell R.A.N. (Ret'd).
16 Selwyn and Sally Jackson
17 Rev I. Beacham
18 Mrs Eileen Fellows
19 ⎫
20 ⎪
21 ⎬ Victor Newburg
22 ⎭
23 Ms Hilary Thistlewood
24 David Smith
25 Ruth Crossley-Holland
26 Mr & Mrs D. Stanners
27 Ann & Bob Elliott
28 Bloxham School
29 S. J. Gale-Botten
30 Jack and Margaret Moore
31 Frank Toole
32 Councillor and Mrs Fred Blackwell
33 Mr & Mrs G. N. Robins
34 Mrs A. H. Greenland
35 R. W. Hobbs
36 R. W. Gilkes
37 D. A. Partridge F.L.A.
38 D. J. Fairbairn
39 Drayton School
40 Mrs L. E. Wright
41 ⎫ Magdalen College
42 ⎭ School
43 Dr & Mrs J. C. Blade
44 North Oxfordshire Technical College
45 Angela Britton
46 P. G. Harris
47 Dr E. R. C. Brinkworth
48 Mrs G. W. Brinkworth
49 M. H. Overfield
50 J. Boss
51 Mrs Trinder
52 C. Hone
53 L. F. Sawyers
54 W. H. Butt

55 Stanbridge Hall Library, Banbury School
56 Mr & Mrs H. R. Clifton
57 Miss Gaby Porter
58 Mr & Mrs J Hall
59 Dr W. Davis
60 Mr & Mrs A. G. Keay
61 William John Vango
62 Geoffrey C. Hartland
63 Mrs R. E. Watts
64 Richard Gaffery
65 Miss Anne Rastall
66 Mr & Mrs K. K. Covill
67 Mr & Mrs D. J. Proctor
68 O. Chaplin
69 Mr & Mrs E. H. Easton
70 Mr & Mrs A. P. Billingham
71 R. J. Major
72 Professor J. N. Buxton
73 Mrs D. O. Durham
74 Miss B. Davis
75 N. R. Hamer
76 D. R. Hancox
77 R. H. Gorton
78 Carol Bateman
79 Mr & Mrs W. N. Richardson
80 R. A. Hubbard
81 Mrs R. S. Bygrave
82 James Bond
83 Mrs Peggy Pike
84 Mrs J. H. J. Medland
85 Mrs Berenice Kent
86 Mrs M. B. Jennens
87 Mrs E. W. Oldfield
88 Leslie Baily F.R.Hist S.
89 Mr & Mrs D. Jarman
90 Mrs C. A. Parsons
91 F. W. Timms
92 P. M. Taylor
93 H. G. Thornton
94 J. T. Foster
95 R. W. Alcock
96 K. C. Baker
97 Jon B. Abbott
98 R. A. C. Mallace
99 S. Brookes
100 Miss T. A. Hughes
101 G. C. Holmes
102 Elizabeth Salby
103 P. N. Emmerson

104 W. J. Nightingale
105 Dr. D. A. Hyslop
106 Peter R. Haley
107 P. P. E. Schroeder
108 D. E. Saint
109 Mr & Mrs G. Batham
110 Mrs R. Huckins
111 L. Tanner
112 W. Gunn
113 Mr & Mrs G. Baker
114 Mr & Mrs M Clews
115 Andy Taylor
116 A. G. Earl
117 Ronald R Bush
118 Dr R. F. Manser
119 Emyr Evans
120 Paul Reed
121 Mrs M. D. Cook
122 Mrs E. T. Abbotts
123 Mrs A. L. Clay
124 ⎫
125 ⎭ Mrs Paul Tator
126 J. R. Davies
127 Paul Spice
128 Gaylord O. Hydal
129 Mrs B. Burns
130 Miss D. Smith
131 Margaret Bickley
132 Paul Moore
133 ⎫
134 ⎭ Malcolm Graham
135 E. Wilkowski
136 E. J. Kahn
137 J. V. Fiori
138 Penny Knowles
139 Mr & Mrs A. Silverwood
140 Mrs H. M. Leach
141 C. G. Stevens
142 C. A. K. Trimbos
143 P. M. Cook
144 T. A. Cox
145 Crispin Paine
146 Dick Smith, B.Sc.
147 Dr Terence Mortimer
148 W. J. Smith
149 A. A. Watt
150 Miss H. E. Bradley
151 Miss H. S. Barbing
152 Miss D. Burrns
153 ⎫
154 ⎭ Mrs M. Davies, M.A.
155 Mr & Mrs P. Callow
156 Mr & Mrs C. Hope

157 Mr & Mrs J. Kenna
158 Mr & Mrs M. Thompson
159 D. J. Barrett
160 Mrs C. Knight
161 G. G. Walker
162 S. A. Withey
163 M. R. Head
164 John D. Ottaway
165 S. A. Eyre
166 A. C. Pennington
167 H. H. Gilkes
168 D. F. Martin
169 Richard A. Stevens
170 E. T. Clark
171 George Fothergill
172 D. N. Tomlinson
173 Sheila M Lee
174 J. G. Duncan
175 Mrs Kuypers
176 Andrew Forbes
177 Herrick R. Dean
178 E. A. Seccull
179 Miss F. M. Stanton
180 R. Cooper
181 Valerie C. Baskwill
182 A. Sargeant
183 T. B. Jones
184 T. H. Byast
185 Sarah Gosling
186 Ival Hornbrook
187 G. H. Feasey
188 Dr Robert Gilchrist
189 Richard Austing
190 Mrs M. L. Garner
191 Miss A. V. Newton
192 Mrs I. M. Blakey
193 Mrs B. Phipps
194 M. F. J. Timlin
195 S. C. W. Mason
196 Mrs M. Cleaver
197 G. Wallington
198 Raymond Boobyer
199 F. A. Beyncowe
200 Miss E. C. Davies
201 Mr & Mrs J. R. Scales
202 Dr Edward S. Stern
203 David G. Ronson
204 P. Skaer
205 H. A. D. Gibbs
206 M. J. Buxton
207 Dr W. Griffel
208 D. A. Hitchcox
209 J. L. Gibbs

210 Dr M. R. Aldous
211 M. Cooling
212 Barry Flanagan
213 Colin Fisher
214 D. Costella
215 B. North
216 Miss B. A. Adkins
217 E. J. Seymour
218 Miss Constance
   Tregurtha
219 Paul Collis
220 Katie Williams
221 Wg Cdr R. L. Smith
222 G. F. Handel
223 Rev Ronald Mitchison
224 Ronnie Hayward
225 F. W. Bolton
226 C. E. Taylor
227 Mrs S. Markham
228 Mrs R. Crossman
229 May Shaw McCloughery
230 Mrs M Viggers
231 Tony Messenger
232 D. J. Griffiths
233 Gillian Beeston
234 Mr & Mrs T. D. Hall
235 Colin Mead
236 Mr & Mrs L. C. Pascoe
237 W. B. Mallett
238 Sally Stradling
239 Drayton Hall Year 3
   Integrated Studies
240 Bob and Betty Rotramel
241 Councillor R. J. Ankers
242 L. Sharman
243 Berkshire College of
   Education
244 P. J. & Mrs J. M.
   Wiltshire
245 Mrs J. M. Bell
246 W. Ramsay
247 G. W. Mumford
248 Gail Canning
249 T. Stone
250 C. E. Boscott
251 Mrs G. M. Weston
252 W. H. Parish
253 K. E. Riley
254 Mrs I. H. Brodey
255 Rev Frank A. White
256 R. T. G. Rice
257 Stella B. Thomas
258 Stuart W. Allsopp
259 Michael Edward Walton
260 Miss Susan Read
261 Mrs Elizabeth A.
   Weedman
262 ⎱ Miss Hilda M. Davis
263 ⎰
264 A. B. Wheeler
265 W. E. Golby
266 Mr & Mrs G. M.
   Wilson
267 Brenda Nutting
268 Nancy Bridges
269 Mrs E. H. Smart
270 Mrs V. G. Barry
271 L. A. Wager
272 Mrs Jeanne Maynard
273 Mrs E. M. M. Shea
274 D. G. Potter
275 Dr R. J. Adam
276 A. H. Phipps
277 Robert Nelder
278 B. Hansford

279 T. Lewis
280 Mrs J. Y. McNaughton
281 H. A. B. White
282 Colin Gilkes
283 K. R. S. Brooks
284 Paul Harris
285 Christine and George
   Lester
286 I. K. Green
287 J. R. Hatton
288 K. French
289 F. S. Mulley
290 Miss Hilary J. Gray
291 Mrs A. Bermingham
292 G. A. Hawkins
293 K. M. Shackleton
294 D. Gilbert
295 Mr & Mrs R. J. Mayne
296 R. F. Beauchamp
297 Mrs I. I. E. Bachelor
298 Miss Jane Barrow
299 J. J. H. Shaw
300 John Saunders
301 Jean Sorenson
302 M. H. Sewin
303 Mrs J. S. Christie
304 Grace E. Sellers
305 Mr & Mrs F. C.
   Buzzard
306 Mr & Mrs A. H. Carter
307 Michael J. Shillington
308 R. Palmer
309 Arthur Coleman
310 Mr & Mrs P. J. Viggers
311 A. T. Williams
312 Peter Chard
313 Denise G. A. Blackwell
314 B. L. Rogers
315 Anon.
316 Barclays Bank Ltd.
317 R. R. J. Hickmett
318 C. N. Kyme
319 Fowlers of Banbury
320 Oxfordshire Probation
   Service
321 E. Gilchrist
322 Stephen & Vicki
   Wegg-Prosser
323 John H. B. Moore
324 Sqn Ldr F. K. Hart
325 Mrs B. Stonehouse
326 R. L. Richards
327 Westminster College
   Library
328 Oxfordshire College of
   Further Education
329 Old Reindeer Inn
330 F. R. Woolam
331 Mrs B. Zocher
332 Whateley Hall Hotel
333 Mrs Tessa English
334 R. A. Upton
335 Bill Cuffley
336 Public Library of Fort
   Wayne and Allen
   County, Indiana
337 Harvard College
   Library
338 J. F. Roberts
339 Dr J. D. Harte
340 F. G. Miller
341 Mrs Mary Clappinson
342 John C. Maycock
343 Miss Mary
   Stanley-Smith

344 Mrs M. C. Walton
345 Guildhall Library
346 ⎱
347 ⎰ Cheney & Sons Ltd
348 ⎰
349 Cdr D. J. Lovell
   Wood RN
350 ⎱
351 ⎰
352 ⎰ Oxfordshire County
353 ⎰ Libraries
354 ⎰
355 Ian B. Madden
356 P. G. Baker
357 Whately Hall
358 Mrs E. M. Robottom
359 A. Robottom
360 Raymond W. Birch
   CBE
361 Mr & Mrs David
   Summers
362 Mrs M. T. Holder
363 Dr Denis B. Woodfield
364 L. A. Fordan
365 A. P. Willis
366 J. St J. Bloxham
367 Capt J. O. N. Wood
368 Beryl and Douglas Jack
369 Thomas Prag
370 John Portergill
371 Ed Salt
372 H. M. Stranks
373 C. G. Castle
374 Mrs J. M. Grubb
375 J. M. Pegler
376 ⎱ Peter W. Lock
377 ⎰
378 Mrs P. Adkins
379 Mrs M. R. Cox
380 F. H. Anker
381 Harold G. Fulcher
382 Mrs Iris Mack
383 Hubert Moller
384 Mrs M. J. Roche
385 Alfred Hartwell
386 P. J. Barrett
387 Clare Appleby
388 ⎱ Mrs D. Dickinson
389 ⎰
390 G. W. Chilton
391 Andrew Railton
392 M. Aldridge
393 G. E. Gardam
394 P. G. Colegrave
395 ⎱ J. T. Lott
396 ⎰
397 Mr & Mrs J. W.
   Looper
398 Mrs I. V. Slinn
399 Geoffrey de C.
   Parmiter
400 R. M. Jacobi
401 M. T. Isham
402 C. J. Bond
403 R. A. E. May
404 F. A. Blencowe
405 Peter Jackson
406 Richard K. French
407 Mary Turnbull
408 D. Bushrod
409 C. A. Warner
410 W. E. Barrett
411 Mrs B. A. Chester-Smith
412 G. L. Nicholson
413 Anne Tofts

414 J. N. Billington
415 B. James
416 J. R. Alcock
417 J. S. W. Gibson
418 J. M. Kite
419 Mrs A. Hart
420 ⎱ Miss M. A. Mascord
421 ⎰
422 J. B. Gordon
423 Susan M. Prentice
424 Mrs Hollamby
425 Mrs Lilian Jean Green
   JP
426 Jennifer Green
427 Diana Green
428 Mrs V. Whiting
429 D. L. Shackleton
430 P. J. Curtis
431 F. J. Taylor
432 Georgina Hampton
433 C. M. Anderson
434 Mrs D. Bentley
435 W. H. Hitchman
436 ⎱ Richard P. Collisson
437 ⎰
438 T. E. Parry
439 Dorothy M. W. Jones
440 Mrs J. K. Adams
441 H. J. Compton
442 John David Duckworth
443 Mr Duff
444 G. R. Tibbetts
445 J. B. Barbour
446 D. E. M. Fiennes
447 Theodore Besterman
448 John William Castle
449 R. K. Gilkes
450 Mrs P. Bradshaw
451 George N. Clark
452 Bishop Loveday School
453 J. H. L. Humphris
454 M. J. Humphris
455 P. Brown
456 R. M. Hancock
457 Valerie Ryman
458 J. Steer
459 P. R. Sutton
460 R. A. Apletree
461 Penny Grimshaw
462 Headmaster, Sibford
   School
463 ⎱ David John Watts
464 ⎰
465 Frank Parry
466 Cleenol Group Ltd.
467 Crest Hotels Ltd.
468 Greatworth Builders Ltd
469 A. Kingston
470 Pharos Lighting
471 Railtons
472 D. A. L. Railton
473 Peter Edward Slinn
474 Malcolm Read
475 David Read
476 F. R. Smith
477 D. G. Vaisey
478 K. E. Lord
479 Dianne Coles
480 D. G. Williams
481 Diana Cunningham
482 Geoff Cox

Remaining names unlisted.

ENDPAPERS:
John Bloxham ARIBA, author's father has recreated the original
Banbury Cross as well as interpreting the cock horse.